Let's all clap hands!

Compiled by Maggie Barfield

Scripture Union, 207–209 Queensway, Bletchley, MK2 2EB, England

© Scripture Union 2001

ISBN 1 85999 528 4

All rights reserved. Permission is granted to photocopy the songs, rhymes and music in *Let's all clap hands!* without reference to current copyright legislation or any copyright licensing scheme. Otherwise, no part of this publication may be reproduced, stored in a retrieval system, or transmitted, in any form or by any means, electronic, mechanical, photocopying, recording or otherwise without the prior permission of Scripture Union.

British Library Cataloguing-in-Publication Data

A catalogue record for this book is available from the British Library.

Cover design by Mark Carpenter Design Consultants

Music setting by Jackie Leigh

Illustrations by Helen Gale

Scripture Union

We are an international Christian charity working with churches in more than 130 countries providing resources to bring the good news about Jesus Christ to children, young people and families – and to encourage them to develop spiritually through the Bible and prayer.

As well as our network of volunteers, staff and associates who run holidays, church-based events and school Christian groups, we produce a wide range of publications and support those who use our resources through training programmes.

Printed and bound by Interprint, Malta

Acknowledgements

Most of the items in this book have appeared in *SALT: 3 to 4+*, *SALT: 5 to 7+*, *SALT: 11 to 13+* and *Sing, say and move* and *Let's join in!* Some previously unpublished material by regular freelance SALT writers is also included.

Thank you to all who have allowed the use of their work. Every effort has been made to attribute items correctly but I apologise to any author whose work has not been properly credited. Please inform the publisher and this will be rectified in any future editions of *Let's all clap hands!*
Maggie Barfield

How to use this book

Suggested actions or sounds are indicated in brackets: (*Wave hands.*)
Lines or verses for all to respond or join in are in bold type: **God is great!**
or italics: *God is great!*

- author
- Bible reference
- tune (suggested well-known melody)
- suggested tips for use

Contents

Why use rhymes and songs? 5

God the maker 6
In the beginning
You made the light
Great and wonderful
Sail little boat
God made
Lights
God's world
Lights for the world
All creatures
We thank you for them all
God made the earth
If God made you
All creatures great and small
God was pleased
Up popped the seeds
God shows his care
Let's all clap hands! (with music)
God does! (with music)
Wherever you are (with music)
Harvest song
Sow the seeds
Seeds and soil
How things grow

God and me 15
Can you breathe?
Body praise!
You are wonderful!
I will sing your praise
Praise for everything!
Alphabet praise
Talking to God
Rest and rap
Who listens?
God knows and cares
Our special friend
The God of surprises!
Sing a new song
God is with me
Trusting God
God will protect us
Talk to God (with music)
God loves you! (with music)
God hears (with music)
Faithful God
Give thanks

Bible people 22
At Mamre
Jacob's dream
Two brothers
Esau and Jacob
Here is Jacob
Who was there?
Sing a song of Jacob
Moses
Moses working
'No', said Pharaoh
Down in Egypt
Over the Red Sea
Leaving Egypt
God is great
So remember (with music)
Only the best (with music)
Through the desert
Manna and water
Hear what God has done
All together
Obey God
God's story
Goliath the giant
Goliath was big
David is sad
If you know who David is
I will miss them
David and Nathan
Solomon's wish
Solomon says
On the mountain
Naaman in the river

Good (not really!) reasons for not using rhymes and songs with children 37
Elisha
The potter's house
Jeremiah and the potter
Jeremiah in the well
Jonah
Jeremiah and the scroll
Go, go Jonah!

Our friend Jesus 41
Day and night
God is good
Jesus is light
Follow him
Jump and sing
Jesus is always with me
I know
Jesus loves us
Listen to the news
You're there!
Good news

Christmas 44
A baby for Elizabeth
Mary's song
An angel came
Ahab was a greedy, greedy king (with music)
Jesus the best friend (with music)
The angels' song
Shepherds on the hill
Camel ride
Christmas animals
Far away
Great wise men
Look up!
Star so bright
Wise men worship

Jesus' life 49
Four busy fishermen
'Come and follow me'
'Follow me!'
Row your boat
Early in the morning
Jesus heals

A man with leprosy
This poor man
Will you come?
At Simon's house
Jairus and Jesus
A daddy and his son
On tiptoe (with music)
The man who was deaf
Helping and healing
Our Father
Bartimaeus
Love
Feeding the five thousand
Ten sick men
Jesus shines!
Wake up!
Shine Jesus
Mary's gift
Mountain top

Stories Jesus told 59

The sower
Do it yourself
The lost son
The farmer and his field
Looking forward (with music)
Sunday comes (with music)
These are the seeds
Little seeds
Looking for the sheep
Seeds
Wise and careless builders
The greatest treasure
Good neighbours?

Easter 66

The donkey's first journey
Red ribbons
Jesus' journey
Bold brave Peter?
Easter morning
Easter

Make your own instruments 69

He's alive
Two friends
Jesus listens
On Easter Day
Jesus is alive!
Three times
Jesus is it you?
Weary fishermen
The promise

The early church 73

Here is the church
The Holy Spirit
Receiving
Peter said
Choose some helpers
Friends
Telling the good news
Stephen
This is Good News
At Pentecost
This way, that way
Yes, yes, yes!

Make your own instruments 77

Come to the church
Let's join in!
Shh!
Read the Bible!
Paul and Silas
Paul's new friends
Paul's travels
Paul's story
God's Spirit
Timothy
Onesimus and Philemon

A child's life 81

God is there!
Why, oh why?
No food
Two busy fathers
This and that
I am growing
Two of us
Superstar!
Who cares?
I don't know
My family
Watching the wind
The library
Art
If you wanna be wise (with music)
Camping out
I like books
Feeling happy
Playing
When I'm sad
Day by day
All I need
Hello God. It's me.
Move it!

Friends 89

Good to see you
Friends
Friends together
When we love you
Sharing friends
What are friends like?
What can friends do together?
Helping friends
Best friends
We hope you'll stay
Hello, hello
Who will be a friend?
Welcome everybody!
Helping

Food and drink 92

Bread for life
Lovely bread
Let the children come (with music)
I'm building a house (with music)
Here and there
My picnic

Index 95

Why use rhymes and songs?

When an 'evil spirit' terrified King Saul, his court officials suggested summoning a young harpist called David and the young man's playing relaxed Saul and made him feel better. (1 Samuel 16:14-23.) When God led the Israelites to freedom through the Red Sea, Moses began the celebrations with a victory song and his sister Miriam organised dancing and tambourines. (Exodus 15:1-21.) And when John wanted to express the essence of who Jesus is, he chose words of power, beauty and poetry. (John 1:1-14.) Many of the best-known and most-loved words in the Bible come to us in the form of songs and poetry.

Most children and adults *enjoy* songs and rhymes. Introducing children to the wonder of music and the delight of words when they are young is a way of giving them access to a resource that will be with them throughout their lives. We can all learn to use our hands and bodies to express rhyme and rhythm. We can develop our skills of listening, interpreting and responding through singing and hearing. Singing, speaking, chanting, dancing – even shouting – give us a shared experience and an opportunity for shared pleasure.

Use songs and rhymes:

As learning experiences

- Songs and rhymes give opportunities for speech practice and voice control, helping children hear and repeat the sound in words more easily.
- They increase children's vocabulary and their understanding of the meaning of words.
- They are good memory exercises.
- They develop confidence and self-esteem.
- They transcend the generation gap.
- Some children (and adults) with speech difficulties find it easier to sing than to speak.

For social development

- 'Music' is usually an activity which everyone does together.
- Songs and rhymes enable children to get to know others and respond to them.
- They enable a child to be known by others and feel part of a group.
- They help the child to respond to the group leader and participate.
- New songs are a link between home and the group: a child may sit quietly and not sing a word but then go home and sing the whole song!
- Singing together, playing an instrument or chanting a rhyme develops cooperation, discipline and self-control.
- They prepare children for moving on to older age groups: by introducing them to rhythmical material, by a leader building on what they already know and by stretching their abilities, imagination and understanding.

As a group activity

- Everyone can be involved.
- Songs and rhymes enable all members of a group to communicate together, through a shared experience.
- Songs and rhymes help to create a group identity.
- They are not demanding.
- They can create a happy and relaxed atmosphere, providing comfort to a frightened or worried child or change the mood of an unhappy or fractious child.
- They can help time pass quickly and cheerfully.
- It costs nothing, needs no resources or equipment and can be done anywhere.

In personal development

Everyone can join in at their own level and at their own pace. A child's involvement could develop like this:

1. Listening.
2. Clapping hands/doing actions.
3. Saying the last word of a line.
4. Singing the chorus.
5. Singing all of the song with everyone else.
6. Insisting on singing the song TO everyone else and expecting applause.
7. Making up new words and different versions of the song.

As a feature of your programme, songs and rhymes can introduce, tell or reinforce a theme, story or biblical truth. They can be a way to remember information or a Bible verse, and even lead to further discussion.

So, **why use songs and rhymes?** Let's go back to where we started and see what answers the Bible gives:

> Shout praises to the LORD! Our God is kind, and it is right and good to sing praises to him. Celebrate and sing!
>
> Play your harps for the LORD our God. The LORD is pleased only with those who worship him
> and trust his love.
>
> Everyone…
>   come and praise the LORD your God!
> (Psalm 147:1,7,11,12)

Let's all clap hands!

God the maker

In the beginning

It was dark – very, very dark,
(Hold up black card.)
Even darker than the darkest night –
But God was there.

It was dark – very, very dark,
(Hold up black card.)
Even darker than the darkest cave –
But God had a plan.

It was dark – very, very dark,
(Hold up black card.)
Even darker than the darkest black –
But then God spoke!

'Let light shine! Bright, bright light!
(Hold up black card.)
Even brighter than the brightest flame.'
God switched it on.

It was light – really, really light,
(Hold up white card.)
Even brighter than the brightest gold.
God said, 'That's good!'

It was light – really, really light,
(Hold up white card.)
Even brighter than the brightest white.
God called it, 'Day'.

It was light – really, really light,
(Hold up white card with gold sun.)
A ball of fire, a wondrous sight.
God called it, 'Sun'.

It was dark, but not so very dark,
(Hold up black card with silver moon.)
A silver ball to give some light.
God called it, 'Moon'.

It was dark, but not so very dark, *(Hold up black card with silver stars.)*
Twinkling lights shone all around.
God called them, 'Stars'.

It was night. *(Hold up black and white card with moon, stars and sun.)*
Then it was day.
Moon and stars. Then sun. Hooray!

And God was pleased.

Jean Elliott

Genesis 1:1-5, 14-19

Creation, sun, moon and stars, lights. Prepare large card shapes: a black square, a white square, a gold sun, silver stars and a silver crescent moon. Hold these up at the beginning of each verse, as suggested. You could give a set of cards to each child so they can hold up the matching cards when the leader demonstrates.

You made the light

Father God you made the light,
Thank you for all you made.
Father God you made the sky,
Thank you for all you made.
You made the sun, you made the moon,
You made the stars that shine.
Father God you made them all
Thank you for all you made.
Yes –
Thank you for all you made.

Maggie Barfield

Genesis 1:1-5, 14-19

a responsive prayer, chant or praise shout

Great and wonderful

Our God, you are great and wonderful.
When we look at the world you have made we know,
Our God, you are great and wonderful.
Children and babies as well as grown-ups want to tell you,
Our God, you are great and wonderful.
When we look at the sky, and see the moon and stars we can see,
Our God, you are great and wonderful.
We thank you for the way you care for us and want to tell you,
Our God, you are great and wonderful.

Elizabeth Alty

exploration of our senses and the variety of the world around us

Sail little boat

Sail little boat 'cross the wide open sea –
Voyage the oceans wide.
See the Lord's power o'er the wind and the waves,
Stirring the rolling tides.
How the storm blows!
How the flood flows!
Waves toss the ship on high!
Sailors cry out –
Desperately shout,
'Lord God! Come, hear our cry!'
Calm is the storm, quiet are the waves.
Safely the ship sails now.
Sailors on board give thanks to the Lord,
Praising him for his power.

Maggie Barfield

Psalm 107:23–30

Speed bonny boat, 'The Skye boat song'

God's world; God's power and protection; natural forces, weather, storms.

God made

God made the ground.
God made clay.
God made sand,
For me to play.

God made compost.
God made peat.
God made leaf mould,
For worms to eat.

God made the land.
God made the earth.
God made the soil,
To give plants birth.

God made flowers.
God made weeds.
God made them grow,
From tiny seeds.

God made all this,
For me to see.
God made our world,
So we should say,
A big thank you!
God, you're good!

Christine Orme

Luke 8:4–15

Hold shakers and give three sharp shakes at the end of each line; everyone can start each line, with a leader adding the item or feature.

God the maker

God the maker

Let's all clap hands!

Lights

Twinkling stars, twinkling stars,
(Open and shut fingers quickly.)
In the night-time sky.
Twinkling stars, twinkling stars,
Twinkling way up high.

Shining moon, shining moon,
(Draw small circles in the air with hands.)
Shining up above.
Shining moon, shining moon,
Tells us of God's love.

Blazing sun, blazing sun,
(Make big sweeping circles with arms.)
Shining all the day.
Blazing sun, blazing sun,
Warms us as we play.

Thank you God, thank you God,
(Arms out sideways.)
For giving us the light.
(Arms raised.)
And thank you God, thank you God,
(Arms out sideways.)
For dark and quiet night.
(Heads bowed, arms down.)

- Geraldine Witcher
- Genesis 1:1-5, 14-19
- Follow the actions suggested; speak quickly and briskly for 'stars'; softly for 'moon'; loudly and cheerfully for 'sun'; and positively for the final verse.

God's world

Long, long ago there was nothing here at all,
Nothing that was big and nothing that was small.
Nothing you could see or taste or touch or smell
But listen and you will hear the wind and water swell.

Clap, tap, ring along with me,
God was thinking hard
Of a world for you and me.
He thought and he thought
Then he spoke out loud,
'There's going to be light
From this dark, dark cloud.'

Light shone brightly from the darkness all around,
The waters roared and the wind blew round and round.
God called the light 'day' and the darkness 'night'
God thought it was good and I think he was right!
Clap, tap ...

God looked all day and he watched through the night,
He had some ideas for the darkness and the light.
He told the moon and stars to brighten up the dark
And the sun to shine brightly in the morning with the lark.
Clap, tap ...

- Dorothy Johnson
- Genesis 1:1-5, 14-19
- Lord of the dance
- Use tambourines, shakers, jingle bells, drums and any other rattle-and-bang instruments and toys you have available; place these on the floor while the verse is sung, then play along with the chorus; teach signals for 'start' and 'stop' and practise before you try this.

Lights for the world

You made the night, you made the day.
Thank you, Jesus, for being the light of the world.
You made the sun, the moon, the stars.
Thank you, Jesus, for being the light of the world.
You made the light shine in the dark.
Thank you, Jesus, for being the light of the world.
You give us light and show us, God.
Thank you, Jesus, for being the light of the world.
You help us shine like lights for you.
Thank you, Jesus, for being the light of the world.

- Jean Elliott
- Genesis 1:1-5, 14-19; John 8:12
- Creation, light, Jesus the light; a responsive chant: divide into two groups or have a leader read alternate lines while everyone says the repeated lines.

All creatures

Thank you, thank you, thank you Lord,
For all creatures big and small.
For the little tiny ant,
For the great big elephant.
Thank you, thank you, thank you Lord,
For all creatures big and small.

Thank you, thank you, thank you Lord,
For all creatures big and small,
For the slowly trailing snail,
For the squirrel's bushy tail.
Thank you, thank you, thank you Lord,
For all creatures big and small.

- Elizabeth Alty
- Genesis 1:20-25
- Twinkle twinkle little star
- Creation, animals; compare the animals by looking at pictures; talk about animals and improvise more verses in the same style, using animals that the children have mentioned.

We thank you for them all

God we praise you
For the animals you made.
The ones that walk,
The ones that crawl -
God we thank you for them all.

God we praise you
For the fishes you have made.
The ones that rush
And swim in shoals -
God we thank you for them all.

God we praise you
For the birds that you have made.
The ones that fly,
The ones that soar -
God we thank you for them all.

- Elizabeth Alty
- Genesis 1:20-25
- All join in the last line of each verse; use the words as a rhyme, a prayer, or as the basis for a mime or music-and-movement activity.
- A way of investigating all the animals God made; play a question, and, answer game and repeat as many times as you can think of animals to mention.

God the maker

God the maker

Let's all clap hands!

God made the earth

Our Lord God, he made the earth,
E-I-E-I-O,
He filled the water with many fish,
E-I-E-I-O,
With a *(Open and close mouth like a fish.)* here,
And a *(Fish.)* there,
Here a *(Fish.)*
There a *(Fish.)*,
Everywhere a *(Fish.)*
Our Lord God, he made the earth,
E-I-E-I-O.

Our Lord God, he made the earth,
E-I-E-I-O,
He filled the air with lots of birds,
E-I-E-I-O,
With a *(Flutter arms like wings.)* here…

Our Lord God, he made the earth,
E-I-E-I-O,
He made all kinds of tame animals,
E-I-E-I-O,
With a purr purr here …

Our Lord God, he made the earth,
E-I-E-I-O,
He made all kinds of wild animals,
E-I-E-I-O,
With a grrr grrr here …

Our Lord God, he made the earth,
E-I-E-I-O,
He made all kinds of small animals,
E-I-E-I-O,
With a squeak squeak here …

Our Lord God, he made the earth,
E-I-E-I-O,
He made all kinds of large animals,
E-I-E-I-O,
With a moo moo here …

Our Lord God, he made the earth,
E-I-E-I-O,
And he was pleased with what he saw,
E-I-E-I-O,
With a big smile here and a big smile there,
Here a smile, there a smile,
Everywhere a big smile,
A moo moo here and a moo moo there,
Here a moo, there a moo,
Everywhere a moo moo,
A squeak, squeak here and a squeak squeak there,
Here a squeak, there a squeak,
Everywhere a squeak squeak,
A grrr grrr here and a grrr grrr there,
Here a grrr, there a grrr,
Everywhere a grrr grrr,
A purr purr here and a purr purr there,
Here a purr, there a purr,
Everywhere a purr purr,
A *(Flutter arms like wings.)* here and a *(Flutter arms like wings.)* there,
Here a *(Flutter arms like wings.)*, there a *(Flutter.)*,
Everywhere a *(Flutter.)*,
A *(Fish)* here
And a *(Fish.)* there,
Here a *(Fish.)*,
There a *(Fish.)*,
Everywhere a *(Fish.)*,
Our Lord God, he made the earth,
E-I-E-I-O!

Lynne Townend

Genesis 1:20–25

Old Macdonald

Follow the pattern of the first verse for all the different creatures God made; add the previous animals in to the end of the verse each time doing actions and making noises, until you end up with the final list! If you make it to the end, you'll need a rest!

If God made you

If God made you and you know it nod your head, *(Nod.)*
If God made you and you know it nod your head, *(Nod.)*
If God made you and you know it then you surely ought to show it,
If God made you and you know it nod your head. *(Nod.)*

If God made you and you know it clap your hands; *(Clap.)*
If God made you and you know it clap your hands; *(Clap.)*
If God made you and you know it then you surely ought to show it,
If God made you and you know it clap your hands. *(Clap.)*

If God made you and you know it jump and hop; *(Jump and hop.)*
If God made you and you know it jump and hop; *(Jump and hop.)*
If God made you and you know it then you surely ought to show it,
If God made you and you know it jump and hop. *(Jump and hop.)*

If God made you and you know it blink your eyes; *(Blink.)*
If God made you and you know it blink your eyes; *(Blink.)*
If God made you and you know it then you surely ought to show it,
If God made you and you know it blink your eyes. *(Blink.)*

If God made you and you know it shout, 'Praise God!'; *(Shout.)*
If God made you and you know it shout, 'Praise God!'; *(Shout.)*
If God made you and you know it then you surely ought to show it,
If God made you and you know it shout, 'Praise God!' *(Shout.)*

If God made you and you know it do all five!
Nod your head, clap your hands, jump and hop, blink your eyes, shout, 'Praise God!' *(Nod, clap, jump and hop, blink, shout.)*
If God made you and you know it do all five!
Nod your head, clap your hands, jump and hop, blink your eyes, shout, 'Praise God!' *(Nod, clap, jump and hop, blink, shout.)*
If God made you and you know it then you surely ought to show it,
If God made you and you know it do all five!
Nod your head, clap your hands, jump and hop, blink your eyes, shout, 'Praise God!' *(Nod, clap, jump and hop, blink, shout.)*

Elizabeth Alty
Genesis 1:26 – 2:4
If you're happy and you know it
Celebrating being God's created people.

Let's all clap hands!

All creatures great and small

On day five *(Hold up fingers and thumb of right hand.)*
God made creatures of the world come alive: *(Wiggle fingers.)*
The fast swimming shark,
(Make a point with index fingers.)
The big octopus,
(Wave arms like tentacles.)
The high flying lark. *(Raise hands as high as you can.)*

On day six *(Hold up six fingers.)*
God made a whole new animal mix.
(Stir hands round and round.)
The tiny tiny flea,
('Bounce' index finger along.)
The wriggly wriggly spider, *('Walk' fingers on one hand along the floor.)*
The buzzy buzzy bee. *(Hold thumb and index forefinger, move around.)*
And at the end of it all, God was pleased! *(Clap loudly.)*

    Elizabeth Alty
    Genesis 1:20-25
    Creation; enjoy impersonating the animals God made.

God was pleased

In the beginning the world was empty
With wide and silent seas.
What living creatures did God make
To fill the earth and skies and trees?

I know, God made the (... *animal*)
And God was very pleased.

    Elizabeth Alty
    Genesis 1:20-25

Up popped the seeds

God made the tiny seeds, hiding in the ground, *(Curl up on the floor.)*
But up popped the seeds, one, two, three, *(Jump up.)*
Up they grew, as tall as you and me, *(Reach up high.)*
And gave us lovely fruit, that helps us jump around! *(Jump and dance.)*

    Angela Thompson
    Genesis 1:11-13
    Creation, growing, plants; act out being the seeds growing into plants.

God shows his care

God shows his care for the land,
By sending rain on the ploughed fields,
And soaking them with water.
He softens the soil with showers,
And makes the young plants grow.
Thank you God!

What a rich harvest his goodness provides.
The fields are filled with flocks;
The hillsides are full of joy.
The valleys are full of wheat.
Everything shouts and sings for joy;
And we do too!
Thank you God!

Paraphrased by: Christine Orme
    Psalm 65:9-13
    God's world, creation, God's provision and care.

God the maker

Let's all clap hands!

Words by Maggie Barfield
Music by Scripture Union

1 Come and sing together, let's all clap hands,
all clap hands, all clap hands. Come and sing together,
let's all clap hands, all clap hands for Jesus.

2 Dance and jump together,
Let's all clap hands,
All clap hands, all clap hands.
Dance and jump together,
Let's all clap hands,
All clap hands for Jesus.

3 Laugh and play together,
Let's all clap hands,
All clap hands, all clap hands.
Laugh and play together,
Let's all clap hands,
All clap hands for Jesus.

© Scripture Union

God does!

Margaret Spivey

1 Who tells a bird to fly, fly, fly? Who tells a fish to swim, swim, swim?
Tells a kangaroo to hop, hop, hop? God does! God does!

2 Who tells a horse to trot, trot, trot?
Who tells a frog to jump, jump, jump?
Tells a chimpanzee to swing, swing, swing?
God does! God does!

3 Who tells a child to grow, grow, grow?
Who tells a child to clap, clap, clap?
Tells us everyone to smile, smile, smile?
God does! God does!

© Margaret Spivey 1998

Wherever you are

Words and music by Mary Irwin-Parker

Wherever you are, whatever you do, remember God is with you too. Wherever you go, you're never alone, God's love will see you through.

© Scripture Union

God the maker

Let's all clap hands!

Harvest song

Sing a song of harvest,
Sing a song today,
All the crops are gathered,
Safely stored away.
Harvest, harvest,
God has given us harvest.
Thank you God for all the food
You give to us today.

- Maggie Barfield
- Sing a song of Maytime
- Parables about growing; celebrating harvest; Jewish harvest festivals.

Sow the seeds

Sow, sow, sow the seeds, everywhere we go, *(Hold hands, dance round.)*
Soon they'll shoot up big and tall, *(Raise hands, still joined.)*
God will grow them. Wow! *(On 'wow' release hands 'explosively'.)*

- Angela Thompson
- Genesis 1:11–13
- Row, row, row your boat
- A praise dance; creation, growing plants, parables of growth.

Seeds and soil

Thank you God
For making seeds.
Thank you God
For different kinds of soil.
Thank you God
For lovely fruit.
Thank you God
For healthy vegetables.
Thank you God
For farmers.
Thank you God
For people who grow our fruit and vegetables.
Thank you God
For our beautiful world.
Please help us to look after it and not spoil it.

- Christine Orme
- Luke 8:4–15
- Cycle of growth, creation, parables about growing, God's provision for our needs. Adapt the prayer to suit your own group, adding ideas from the children.

How things grow

Father God, we want to say thank you for sending rain so that the plants have enough water to drink. *(Move shakers gently.)*
Thank you for sending the sun *(Hold up the sun shape, smile.)* to warm the soil so that seeds can sprout. *(Curl up like seeds then start to grow.)*
Thank you for giving light so that plants have healthy, green leaves. *(Stretch upwards.)*
Thank you for the farmers *(Mime sowing, digging, driving tractor.)* and everybody who works hard to grow food for us to eat.
For rain, sun, sprouting seeds, growing plants, and farmers who work hard to grow our food, we want to say, 'Thank you, Father God.'

- Kathleen Crawford
- Luke 8:4–15
- An action prayer about growth cycle of plants. Use shakers and a large sun shape cut from yellow card or paper.

God and me

Can you breathe?

Can you breathe?
YES!
Then praise the Lord.
Can you breathe?
YES!
Then praise the Lord.
Can you breathe?
YES!
Then praise the Lord,
Praise the Lord.
Praise the Lord,
Praise the Lord!

Everybody praise the Lord.
If you can breathe then praise the Lord.
Everybody praise the Lord.
Everybody praise the Lord.

We can praise the Lord together.
If you can breathe then praise the Lord.
We can praise him on our own.
Everybody praise the Lord.

Praise the Lord when we're together.
If you can breathe then praise the Lord.
Praise the Lord when we're at home.
Everybody praise the Lord.

We can praise him with our music.
If you can breathe then praise the Lord.
We can praise him with our songs.
Everybody praise the Lord.

Praise God for the love he's shown us.
If you can breathe then praise the Lord.
Praise for what he's going to do.
Everybody praise the Lord.

Everybody praise the Lord.
If you can breathe then praise the Lord.
Everybody praise the Lord.
Everybody praise the Lord.

Can you breathe?
YES!
Then praise the Lord!
Can you breathe?
YES!
Then praise the Lord!
Can you breathe?
YES!
Then praise the Lord,
Praise the Lord.
Praise the Lord,
Praise the Lord!

Jonathan Gower
Psalms 149, 150
A praise chant, with responses

Body praise!

I could praise God all day long
With my mouth, with my mouth. *(Point to mouth.)*
I could praise God all day long
Because I know he loves me. *(Stretch arms upward and then in towards yourself.)*

Christine Wright
Acts 3:1–10
Repeat the prayer using a different part of the body, adapting your actions to match.

Let's all clap hands

You are wonderful!

I will praise you my God and King,
You are wonderful Lord.
You make me want to shout and sing,
You are wonderful Lord.
Old and young will give you praise,
You are wonderful Lord.
All the world will tell your ways,
You are wonderful Lord.
You are good to everyone,
You are wonderful Lord.
Plants, trees, animals, moon and sun,
You are wonderful Lord.
You give us all the things we need,
You are wonderful Lord.
And everything you do is good,
You are wonderful Lord.
I will praise you my God and King,
You are wonderful Lord.
You make me want to shout and sing,
You are wonderful Lord.

- Claire Saunders
- Psalm 145
- A praise chant, with response.

I will sing your praise

Always and forever I will sing your praise,
Because you are wonderful in all your ways.

Children, grown-ups, young and old,
Delight to hear your greatness told.

Every nation all over the world,
From every corner their praise is heard.

Great and small in all creation
Hear and join the celebration.

It's good to feel you're always there,
Joyful times, sad times – you help and care.

Always and forever I will sing your praise,
Because you are wonderful in all your ways.

- Claire Saunders
- Psalm 145
- An acrostic praise poem based on an acrostic psalm. Originally written to celebrate the new millennium.

Praise for everything!

Clap, clap, clap your hands,
Clap your hands and sing,
We can clap to praise you God,
Praise for everything!

Wave, wave, wave your hands,
Wave your hands and sing,
We can wave to praise you God,
Praise for everything!

Play, play, play the tune,
Play the tune and sing,
We can play to praise you God,
Praise for everything!

- Alison Gidney
- Mark 3:1-6
- Row row row your boat
- Trying different ways to praise God; improvise actions to each verse.

Alphabet praise

All creation is God's work,
Praise the Lord who was, who is and is to come.
Blessed are we who believe in him,
Praise the Lord who was, who is and is to come.
Come to him with shouts of joy,
Praise the Lord who was, who is and is to come.
Deep is his love for us,
Praise the Lord who was, who is and is to come.
Everything on earth was made by him,
Praise the Lord who was, who is and is to come.
Follow him with a joyful heart,
Praise the Lord who was, who is and is to come.
Great is his name,
Praise the Lord who was, who is and is to come.
He sends his Holy Spirit to us,
Praise the Lord who was, who is and is to come.
In everything he is with us,
Praise the Lord who was, who is and is to come.
Jesus was sent by him to be our saviour,
Praise the Lord who was, who is and is to come.
King over all the nations,
Praise the Lord who was, who is and is to come.
Lovingly he cares for us,
Praise the Lord who was, who is and is to come.
Mercy and kindness are his,
Praise the Lord who was, who is and is to come.
No one can compare to him,
Praise the Lord who was, who is and is to come.
Only worship him,
Praise the Lord who was, who is and is to come.
Praise the Lord, Amen.

- Clive de Salis
- Psalm 145
- An acrostic poem based on an acrostic psalm; originally written to celebrate the new millennium; all join in the repeated line of this praise chant or responsive prayer.

Talking to God

God wants us to talk to him.
What shall we say?
'Praise God, you are very great in every way.'

God wants us to talk to him.
What shall we say?
'Please give us the things we need just for today.'

God wants us to talk to him.
What shall we say?
'We're sorry that we do wrong things and disobey.'

God wants us to talk to him.
What shall we say?
'Please help us to live for you all through each day.'

- Jacquie Sibley
- Matthew 6:5–15
- A question-and-answer rhyme version of the Lord's Prayer.

God and me

God and me

Let's all clap hands!

Rest and rap

In the beginning God created the lot.
He worked really hard for six days on the trot.
On the seventh day, God decided to rest.
He said working six days and then resting was best.

God made man to do the same.
We like to keep busy, that's part of the game.
But God says we should take time to unwind.
One day a week we should turn from the grind.

Keep one day special to worship the Lord,
To meet together and to study his word.

Jesus had real power, a dynamic force,
But he still took time to get back to the source.
Just him and God, on a one to one;
Some serious talking had to be done.

If God's Son Jesus had to take time out,
Then so do we, without a doubt.
So you'd better remember to keep one day
On which you make time to rest and pray.

Keep one day special to worship the Lord,
To meet together and to study his word.

Mandy Engelsma

Genesis 2:2-4; Psalm 23; Mark 6:30-32; Leviticus 23:3

Creation, resting, time for God; speak using a rap rhythm, keeping time by clapping; encourage all to join in with 'Keep one day…'

Who listens?

When the world is wonderful and we are happy, who listens to us?
My God always listens to what I have to say,
Every single moment of every single day.

When we are ill or sad or lonely, who listens to us?
My God always listens to what I have to say,
Every single moment of every single day.

When we are frightened or nervous or feel silly, and we don't know what to do, who listens to us?
My God always listens to what I have to say,
Every single moment of every single day.

When everyone the whole world over is praying, who listens to us?
My God always listens to what I have to say,
Every single moment of every single day.

Rose Williams

Matthew 7:7-12

A responsive prayer; add more 'When' lines based on discussions with your group.

God knows and cares

God knows us all, everybody. *(Children point to one another.)*
God knows us all.
Let's sing his praise, Hallelujah! *(Children clap.)*
Let's sing his praise.

God cares for us, everybody. *(Children point again.)*
God cares for us.
Let's sing his praise, Hallelujah! *(Children clap again.)*
Let's sing his praise.

- Jacquie Sibley
- Acts
- Lavender's Blue
- The lilting tune of this song gives a feeling of security; it's fine to praise and worship gently, as well as enthusiastically.

Our special friend

Children, grown-ups, all praise Jesus.
Jesus is our special friend.
Jesus loves to hear us talking.
Jesus is our special friend.
Jesus loves to see us playing
Jesus is our special friend.
And his love will never end.
Jesus is our special friend.

- Christine Wright
- Luke 18:15-17
- A responsive rhyme or prayer; say it loudly and cheerfully as a praise chant; or more quietly and reflectively to reinforce the words. You could use the prayer more than once in a session, using the same words but different worship style.

The God of surprises!

He's the God of surprises! *('Yeah, yeah!')*
He's the God of us all. *(Point around the circle.)*
He's the God who chose David
Though he was young and small. *('Let's praise him!')*

He's the God of surprises! *('Yeah, yeah!')*
He's the God of us all. *(Point around the circle.)*
He's the God who has chosen ME *(Shout.)*
Though I am young and small. *('Praise him!')*

- Helen Burn
- 1 Samuel 16:1-13
- 'Who's the king of the jungle?'
- Being special to God and chosen by him; suggested actions given in brackets.

Sing a new song

Sing a new song to the Lord,
We'll sing a new song to the Lord,
Sing a new song, sing a new song,
Sing a new song to the Lord.

- Margaret Spivey
- Luke 2:36-38
- Hickory dickory dock
- With most Bible stories and themes.

God and me

Let's all clap hands!

God is with me

Father God, when sudden, loud noises give me a fright,
You are with me and I can be brave.

When lightning flashes and thunder rumbles,
You are with me and I can be brave.

When ordinary things look much different in the dark,
You are with me and I can be brave.

When children much bigger than me are rushing around,
You are with me and I can be brave.

When I meet lots of people I've never seen before,
You are with me and I can be brave.

Wherever I go, whatever I do, thank you God that
You are with me and I can be brave.

- Kathleen Crawford
- 1 Samuel 17:1-58
- All say the repeated line, to assure and reassure children of God's constant presence with us. Add more verses based on children's own suggestions but always end with the final stanza.

Trusting God

When I'm troubled, God, you listen
To my prayer, to my praise.
You bless me when I trust you,
You're kind to all who call you,
Thank you God, thank you God.

I obey you, I will trust you
With my life, with my plans.
I know you care about me,
I can't live without you,
Thank you God, thank you God.

- Elizabeth Alty
- Psalm 40:1-11
- Frère Jacques
- A prayer or song of dedication.

God will protect us

You, O Lord, are always my shield from danger.
Thank you God that you will always protect us.
O Lord, our Lord your greatness is seen in all the world.
Thank you God that you will always protect us.
I trust in the Lord for safety.
Thank you God that you will always protect us.
May the Lord answer you when you are in trouble.
Thank you God that you will always protect us.
The Lord is my Shepherd, I have everything I need.
Thank you God that you will always protect us.
To you, O Lord, I offer my prayer; in you, my God, I trust.
Thank you God that you will always protect us.

- Malc' Halliday
- Words from psalms, used with story of David 1 Samuel 19:11-12; 20; 23:14-18
- To assure children of God's power and protection for us. Make the link between psalms written long ago and the application for today: God will protect us now just as he protected David long ago.

Talk to God

Words by Christine Wright
Music by Maggie Barfield

Brightly

Talk, talk, talk to God, and tell him what you need.
('Talk' using hand.)
Wait, wait, wait for God, he'll listen, yes indeed.
(Hand behind ear.)
Talk, talk, talk to God, and
('Talk' using hand.)
say what's on your mind. Listen to God. He's loving, good and kind.
(Hand behind ear.)

© Scripture Union

God loves you!

Words by Elizabeth Alty
Music by Scripture Union

1 When you're feeling sad and blue and you don't know what to do, Here's a message to see you through, God loves you!

2 When you know that you've been bad
And you've made somebody sad,
Here's a message to make you glad,
God loves you!

3 When you feel you're on your own
And your friends have been and gone,
Here's a message, you're not alone,
God loves you!

4 In all kinds of places you must know
God sees and cares wherever you go.
Here's a message that you can show,
God loves you!

© Scripture Union

God hears

Words by Elizabeth Alty
Music by ER Hooke

God hears when I speak,
(Cup ear, point to mouth.)
God listens when I
(Cup ear, point to mouth.)
talk to him. He hears my cry,
(Cup ear, then mouth.)
knows what I need. I'm
(Hands outstretched.)
glad God listens to me. I'm glad God listens to me.
(Point to self.) *(Point to self.)*

© ER Hooke 1990

Let's all clap hands!

21

Let's all clap hands!

Faithful God

Faithful are you, O God, and your love is strong.
My heart is full of thanks. I'll praise you the whole day long.
I called you when I was sad, happiness came from you.
Wonderful is your name, your promises always come true!

- Mary Houlgate
- Psalm 138
- Here we go Looby-lou
- A song of praise; sing twice through, then play or hum the tune while children dance freely; then repeat the song again.

Give thanks

Give thanks to the Lord, for he is good,
His love lasts for ever!
Give thanks to the God of gods,
His love lasts for ever!
Give thanks to the Lord of lords,
His love lasts for ever!
By his wisdom he made the heavens,
His love lasts for ever!
He built the earth on the deep waters,
His love lasts for ever!
He made the sun and the moon,
His love lasts for ever!
Give thanks to the God of heaven,
His love lasts for ever!

- Christine Orme
- Psalm 136:1–3, 5, 9, 26
- A responsive rhyme, prayer or praise shout.

Bible people

At Mamre

Underneath the spreading terebinth tree,
Sarah was surprised to see,
Three strange men had come to tea,
'Neath the spreading terebinth tree.

'God sent us with news to tell you two,
A baby will be born to you,
Please believe us; it is true,
Nothing is too hard for God to do!'

Underneath the spreading terebinth tree,
Sarah laughed and laughed with glee,
'A baby boy for you and me!
Oh! How happy we will be!'

- Maggie Barfield
- Genesis 18:1–16
- Underneath the spreading chestnut tree
- Abraham had a semi-permanent camp in the hill-country around Mamre where there were sacred terebinth trees; these were spreading trees about 7-8m high which were common in warm, dry, hilly areas. Children can act out being the trees, stretching arms out wide and waving branches.

Jacob's dream

Poor Jacob's feeling lonely, he's so sad and frightened,
Poor Jacob's feeling lonely, he's all on his own.

He's going on a journey, a very long journey,
He's going on a journey, a long way from home.

Bible people

He has to go to sleep now, his pillow's a hard stone,
He has to go to sleep now, so far from his home.

But Jacob dreams of angels and stairs up to heaven.
God says to dreaming Jacob, 'You're NOT on your own.'

God says, 'I love you Jacob, and I'll never leave you;
I'll take care of you always and bring you back home.'

Jacob wakes up happy, not lonely, not frightened;
He knows God's always with him. He's NOT all alone!

- Christine Orme
- Genesis 28:10–22
- Poor Mary sits a-weeping
- Walk round in a circle, changing direction after each two lines.

Two brothers

Esau: 'Who was born holding my heel?
Who never cares how I might feel?
Who tricked me when I needed a meal?
My brother!'

Jacob: 'Who makes me cross 'cos he's older than me?
Who's as hairy as can be?
Who did I trick when he wanted his tea?
My brother!'

Esau: 'Who does Mum like best of all?
Who has smooth skin and looks so cool?
Who took my blessing and made <u>me</u> look a fool?
My brother!'

Jacob: Who's so cross, I've had to leave home?
Who won't care wherever I roam?
Who'll be glad I've left him alone?
My brother!'

Together: 'Oh, I *wish* we could be friends!'

Jacob: 'Who did I meet as I travelled today?
Who came and hugged me and asked me to stay?
Who made me happier than I can ever say?
My brother!'

Esau: 'Who came travelling through my land?
Who sent me camels and goats and lambs?
Who bowed down and shook my hand?
My brother!'

Together: 'Oh, thank you, God! We're friends at last!'

- Jean Elliott
- Life of Jacob
- 'My brother!' comic song
- Divide the children into two groups, one being Esau and the other Jacob. Read the appropriate verses of the poem. If your younger children cannot read well, let them join in enthusiastically with the last line of each verse.

Let's all clap hands!

Esau and Jacob

Isaac and Rebekah had twin baby boys,
Isaac and Rebekah had twin baby boys.
Esau was the elder one, Jacob was the younger son,
Isaac and Rebekah had twin baby boys.

As they grew up they liked doing different things,
As they grew up they liked doing different things,
Esau liked to hunt for meat, Jacob cooked good things to eat.
As they grew up they liked doing different things.

Jacob wished that he could be the elder son,
Jacob wished that he could be the elder son,
Esau was so hungry one day that he gave his blessing away.
Jacob wished that he could be the elder son.

Jacob played a sneaky trick on his old dad,
Jacob played a sneaky trick on his old dad,
He put on some hairy skins and he stole Esau's blessing.
Jacob played a sneaky trick on his old dad.

Esau was so cross, he said 'I'll kill that boy.'
Esau was so cross, he said 'I'll kill that boy.'
At home he could not stay so Jacob had to run away.
Esau was so cross, he said 'I'll kill that boy.'

Helen Burn
Genesis 25:19-34; 27:1-45
If you're happy and you know it
Use the song to tell and re-enact the story.

Here is Jacob

Here is brother Jacob,
(Hold up forefinger of one hand.)
Here is brother Esau,
(Hold up forefinger of other hand.)
Living in a tent, *(Make sloping tent shape above head with both hands.)*
One day they quarrel,
(Clench fists and pummel air.)
Oh dear, dear, dear,
(Shake head sadly.)
Jacob has to go away.
(Make fingers walk.)

Here is brother Jacob,
(Hold up forefinger.)
Going on a journey,
(Make fingers walk.)
Feeling scared and lonely. *(Hunch shoulders, look sad and fearful.)*
Then he has a good dream, *(Head on hands, close eyes and smile.)*
God says, 'I'll look after you!'
(Bring arms round to front as if protecting someone.)
Jacob wakes up happy!
(Mime waking up and smiling.)

Jacob stayed with Uncle Laban.
(Hold up forefinger.)
Married Leah and Rachel, *(Circle third finger of left hand for wedding ring.)*
They had lots of babies, *(Rock babies.)*
Lots of animals too, *(Make animal ears with hands on head.)*

'Thank you God!' said Jacob,
(Hands together as if praying.)
'I'm so happy now!'
(Indicate smiley face with fingers.)

But Jacob remembered
(Hold up forefinger, then touch temple and frown slightly.)
His home and his brother.
(Make tent shape and hold up other finger for Esau.)
He wanted to see them again.
(Cross arms on chest.)
Got up on the camels,
(Mime holding reins and riding.)
Said sorry to Esau, *(Open hands upwards and look sorry.)*
And then the brothers were friends!
(Clap.)

Christine Orme

Genesis 25–33

Follow the suggested actions and use this rhyme to tell the whole life story of Jacob. Choose particular verses to match the part of the story you are telling.

Who was there?

When things went wrong for Joseph,
When his brothers called him names,
When they sold him to the traders,
When he ended up a slave,
When he was put in prison
When he was forgotten there –
   Who was there?
   GOD WAS THERE!

When things went well for Joseph,
When the king became his friend,
When his brothers came to see him,
When they made up in the end,
When the family moved to Egypt,
When they learned to care and share –
   Who was there?
   GOD WAS THERE!

Maggie Barfield

Genesis 37, 39–47

Contrast the positive and negative events of the life of Joseph; use with 'God is there!' in 'A Child's life' page 81 where children's experiences are compared and contrasted.

Sing a song of Jacob

Sing a song of Jacob, walking all alone,
Sleeping on the ground with a pillow made of stone.
Sing a song of Jacob, listening to God say,
'Cheer up! I am with you, and I'll bring you home one day.'

Sing a song of Jacob in his uncle's home,
Wives called Leah and Rachel and children of his own.
Sing a song of Jacob setting off to say,
'I'm sorry, brother Esau, let's be good friends from today.'

Christine Orme

Genesis 25–33

Sing a song of sixpence

An overview of the life of Jacob.

Bible people

Bible people

Let's all clap hands!

Moses

Moses in a basket,
Floating on the water,
Someone came and found him,
It was the king's daughter!
Little baby Moses,
Grew up tall and strong,
But he had to run away
When he did something wrong.

Moses in the desert,
With his sheep and goats,
Saw a bush on fire,
Listened when God spoke,
'Listen to me Moses.
To Egypt you must go
And tell the king of Egypt
He must let my people go!'

See God's people travelling,
To a brand new land,
Hungry, tired and thirsty,
Walking in the sand.
God sends food from heaven,
Manna they can eat,
And when Moses hits the rock,
Clean water, cold and sweet!

- Christine Orme
- Exodus
- Sing a song of sixpence
- Use the whole song to give an overview of the life of Moses or choose individual verses, as appropriate.

Moses working

Moses working, Moses working,
Far away, far away,
God sent him a message, God sent him a message,
Listen please, listen please.

'Go to Egypt, go to Egypt,
Tell the king, tell the king.
You must be the leader, you must be the leader,
Of my people, of my people.'

'I can't do it, I can't do it.
I am scared, I am scared.'
'I will be with you, I will be with you,
Off you go, off you go.'

'They won't believe me, they won't believe me,
I am scared, I am scared.'
'I will be with you, I will be with you,
Off you go, off you go.'

'I'm no good at speaking, I'm no good at speaking,
I am scared, I am scared.'
'I will be with you, I will be with you,
Off you go, off you go.'

'Send someone else, send someone else,
I am scared, I am scared.'
'I will be with you, I will be with you,
Off you go, off you go.'

- Formerly in *Sing, say and move*
- Exodus 3:1–12
- Frère Jacques
- From verse three onwards, the children could divide into two groups; one to sing Moses' words and the other to sing God's words. Or the song can be taught quickly as an echo song, with the leader singing each phrase the first time and everyone repeating it.

'No,' said Pharaoh

God says 'Let my people go!' said Moses to the proud Pharaoh.
'No,' said Pharaoh, 'the people can't go.'

So first the river turned blood red;
The people couldn't drink, and the fishes soon were dead.
The frogs leapt out and jumped around.
Soon there wasn't anywhere they couldn't be found.
But 'No,' said Pharaoh, 'the people can't go.'

Soon there were gnats and flies buzzing in the air,
Biting all the people and getting in their hair.
And the Egyptian animals grew sick and died,
And the people's skin so sore that they couldn't go outside.
But 'No,' said Pharaoh, 'the people can't go.'

Then came the hail and it flattened all the wheat,
And the locusts came and ate the rest till there was nothing left to eat.
Then everywhere went dark and the sun refused to shine.
But 'No,' said Pharaoh, 'the people can't go.
I want them to be mine!'

Alison Gidney

Exodus 3–10

The story of the plagues and Pharaoh's obstinacy; add improvised actions, acting out the different types of plague and shaking heads and wagging fingers each time Pharaoh speaks.

Down in Egypt

The frogs on the land go hop, hop, hop,
hop, hop, hop,
hop, hop, hop
The frogs on the land go hop, hop, hop,
All day long.

The flies in the air go buzz, buzz, buzz,
buzz, buzz, buzz, buzz, buzz, buzz,
The flies in the air go buzz, buzz, buzz,
All day long.

The people with the sores go moan, moan, moan,
moan, moan, moan, moan, moan,
The people with the sores go moan, moan, moan,
All day long.

The hail from the skies goes crash, crash, crash,
crash, crash, crash, crash, crash,
The hail from the skies goes crash, crash, crash,
All day long.

The locusts on the wheat go munch, munch, munch,
munch, munch, munch,
munch, munch, munch,
The locusts on the wheat go munch, munch, munch,
All day long.

Then everything goes dark as dark can be, dark can be, dark can be,
Then everything goes dark as dark can be,
All day long.

But God takes care of his people I know, people I know, people I know,
But God takes care of his people I know,
All day long.

Alison Gidney

Exodus 7–10

The wheels on the bus

Enjoy adding sound effects and actions to this song; older children and adults enjoy joining in with this song in all-age worship!

Bible people

Let's all clap hands!

Over the Red Sea

God made a path right through the sea,
Thank you, thank you, God!
God made a path right through the sea,
Thank you, thank you, God!
The wind blew here and the wind blew there, here a puff, there a puff, everywhere a puff, puff –
God made a path right through the sea,
Thank you, thank you God!

- Christine Orme
- Exodus 14
- Old Macdonald had a farm
- Younger children will find it easy to join in with parts of this song to a familiar tune, while everyone can blow as hard as they can and see if they can blow the sea aside!

Leaving Egypt

'Go, go!' went Pharaoh,
'Quick, quick!' went Moses,
'Waa-waa!' went the babies,
'Yippee!' went the children,
As God's people left Egypt.

Baa, baa, went the sheep,
Maa, maa, went the goats,
Eeee-aaw, went the donkeys,
Woof, woof, went the dogs,
As God's people left Egypt.

Buzz, buzz, went the flies,
Chirp, chirp, went the grasshoppers,
Flip, flop, went the feet,
Swish, swish, went the sand,
As God's people left Egypt.

Left right, went the soldiers,
Clip clop, went the horses,
Moan, moan, went the people,
'Don't worry,' went Moses,
As God's people reached the Red Sea.

Whoosh, whoosh, went the wind,
Splish, splash, went the sea,
'Look, look,' went the people,
Crunch, crunch, went the path,
As God's people crossed the Red Sea.

'God's great!' went Moses,
'Yes he is!' went the people,
'God saved us!' went the fathers,
'Sing to God!' went Miriam,
When God's people crossed the Red Sea.

- Christine Orme
- Exodus 14
- A sound effects rhyme, giving plenty of scope for interaction and involvement; leader calls out each line and pauses while everyone makes appropriate noises. For all-age worship, hand out cards with one line on each so that everyone in the congregation has one; remind everyone to listen closely, then read the rhyme through with groups of people making the noise on their card.

God is great

I will sing to God because he's the winner!
He is the one who kept me safe!
He is my God and I will praise him,
And sing about his greatness!
You are very great, Lord! (x3)

You blew on the sea and the water piled up high,
It stood up straight like a wall.
Oh Lord there is no one like you!
You are king for ever and ever!
You are very great, Lord! (x3)

- Christine Orme
- Exodus 15
- A praise chant for two voices, two groups, or a leader and group.

So remember

Deuteronomy 4:1–14

Music by Nick Harding

Fast

So remember today and never forget, the Lord is God in heaven and earth. So remember today and never forget, the Lord is God in heaven and earth.

© Nick Harding

Only the best

Words and music by Sue Dunn

1 When Solomon decided to build the temple, he wanted it as fine as it could be. So he sent a message to the king of Tyre, saying, 'Send all your best wood to me. Only the best is good enough for God, so send all your best wood to me.'

2 When Solomon decided to build the temple,
He wanted it as strong as it could be.
So he sent his workers into the hills,
Saying, 'Cut all the best stone for me.
Only the best is good enough for God,
So cut all the best stone for me.'

3 When Solomon decided to build the temple,
He wanted it as beautiful as could be.
So he covered it all over with gold so bright,
Saying, 'God has been so good to me.
Only the best is good enough for God,
For God has been so good to me.'

© Scripture Union

Let's all clap hands

Bible people

Let's all clap hands!

Through the desert

We have to get things ready,
(Sort out and pack.)
We're going on a journey.
We've got to eat a special meal,
(Mime eating.)
We're going on a journey.
It's going to be a long one,
(Make twisty movements of hand and arm to show length.)
We're going on a journey.
A journey to a new land,
(Thumbs up.)
We're going on a journey.
With sheep and goats and donkeys,
(Make animal noises and wiggle hands as 'ears'.)
We're going on a journey.
Following God's big cloud,
(Make cloud shape with hands.)
We're going on a journey.
It's hot and dry and dusty, (Mop brow.)
We're going on a journey.
And now we've reached the Red Sea,
(Make waves with hands.)
We're going on a journey.
Oh no – here come the soldiers,
(Look anxious, mime galloping.)
We're going on a journey.
We're very cross with Moses!
(Fold arms, look angry, shake fists.)
We're going on a journey.
We're stuck here at the Red Sea,
(Look all round, shrug, hold palms up.)
We're going on a journey.
Whatever's Moses doing now?
(Stretch out hand as if over sea.)
We're going on a journey.
Oh –.can you hear the wind blow?
(Make blowing noises and sway.)
We're going on a journey.
LOOK! A path through the sea!
(Point excitedly.)
We're going on a journey.
We're walking through the sea!
(Walk on spot, look at of walls water.)
We're going on a journey.
God's helped us cross the Red Sea,
(Shake heads in amazement.)
We're going on a journey.
But first we're going to praise God,
(Jump up and down, clap, dance about.)
We're going on a journey.
Hooray, hooray!

Christine Orme

Exodus 14, 15

Tell and act out the story, with everyone joining in the actions and saying the repeated line; this will reinforce the 'journey' motif, even if children do not grasp every incident of the story.

Manna and water

(Stand in a ring and walk round holding hands.)
The Israelites lived long ago, long ago, long ago,
The Israelites lived long ago, long ago.

(March on the spot with one finger pointing forwards.)
Moses led them to the desert, to the desert, to the desert,
Moses led them to the desert, to the desert.

(Look around for water and shrug shoulders.)
They could not find water there, water there, water there,
They could not find water there, water there.

(Kneel on the floor and beat fists on the ground.)
The people moaned and moaned and moaned, moaned and moaned, moaned and moaned,
The people moaned and moaned and moaned, moaned and moaned.

(Stay kneeling and act as if praying.)
Then Moses cried out to the Lord, to the Lord, to the Lord,
Then Moses cried out to the Lord, to the Lord.

(Stand up and act having a drink.)
The Lord God gave them water to drink, water to drink, water to drink,
The Lord God gave them water to drink, water to drink.

(Kneel on the floor and beat fists on the ground.)
The people moaned that they had no food, had no food, had no food,
The people moaned that they had no food, had no food.

(Walk around gathering food in pretend baskets.)
The Lord God gave them bread from heaven, bread from heaven, bread from heaven,
The Lord God gave them bread from heaven, bread from heaven.

(Walk around in a ring holding hands.)
The Israelites lived long ago, long ago, long ago,
The Israelites lived long ago, long ago.

Rachael Champness

Exodus 16

There was a Princess long ago

Act out living in desert conditions while you sing this song.

Hear what God has done

This is what God has done and we must tell the children.
Don't forget all that he has done for you.
The Lord has done amazing things!
He divided the sea and led his people through it.
He guided them with the cloud by day and with light from the fire all night.
He gave them water, as much as in the seas.
God gave manna for the people to eat.
The people remembered that God was their Rock.
He is our God too. Hooray! Let's praise him!

Rachael Champness

Psalm 78; Exodus 15-17

Review the events of the exodus with this adaptation from psalms.

All together

All together, all together,
We all share in God's story.
All the Israelites and Moses
Have a part, and so do we.

Helen Burn

Deuteronomy 4:32-40

Clementine

God's involvement with his people did not stop when the Bible was complete: this song affirms that we are part of God's ongoing relationship with humanity.

Bible people

Let's all clap hands!

Obey God

The Lord gives us everything we need.
Obey his commands –
Lord, help us to obey.
The Lord is the only one to worship.
Put him first in everything –
Lord, help us to obey.
If we obey God, other people will notice and ask questions –
Lord, help us to obey.
Do not forget the things God has done for us.
Pass them on to others –
Lord, help us to obey.
Lord, help us to obey.

Nick Harding
Deuteronomy 4:1–14
A responsive prayer to help us identify with the message Moses gave to the people of God.

God's story

God helped his people long ago
And he helps us too wherever we go.
We're in the story!
It's God's story!

When we're scared or running away
God helps us out and finds a way.
We're in the story!
It's God's story!

God gave Moses rules for living.
They're our rules too for loving and giving.
We're in God's story!
It's OUR story!

Helen Burn
Deuteronomy 4:32–40

God's involvement with his people did not stop when the Bible was complete: this rhyme affirms that we are part of God's ongoing relationship with humanity.

Goliath the giant

Goliath was a giant who was tall, tall, tall,
He laughed at David who was small, small, small.
'Come out and fight me if you dare, dare, dare;
I'm stronger than a lion or a bear, bear, bear!'

Young David was a shepherd who was brave, brave, brave.
'I'll rely on God and he will save, save, save.'
He felt in his pocket for his sling, sling, sling,
And a stone flew through the air with a zing, zing, zing.

Maggie Barfield
1 Samuel 17
Miss Polly had a dolly
Clap briskly three times as you repeat the final word of each line.

Goliath was big

Goliath was big *(Arms outstretched)*,
Goliath was tall *(Reach up with one arm.)*,
He was the strongest *(Fists clenched, arms bent up at elbows)* soldier of all.
(Pretend to sword fight.)

David was young *(Smile.)*, David was small, *(Indicate own height.)*
David was not a soldier at all.
(Shake head from side to side.)

Goliath laughed and laughed 'But, he's only a lad,
This is the easiest fight I've ever had.
He's got no armour, no sword and no spear,
What have I, the great champion, got to fear?'
Goliath was big …

David said, 'No lions or bears are a problem for me,
As for giant Goliath – well, he'll soon see
That he may have strength and power and might,
But with God's help I know I'll win this fight.'
Goliath was big …

Goliath wore bronze armour, had a sword, shield and spear,
He laughed as he waited for David to appear.
David swung his sling with a stone he had found
And the giant Goliath fell down on the ground.
Goliath was big …

Kathleen Crawford

1 Samuel 17

Tell the story with this rhyme, repeating the chorus and doing the suggested actions after each verse.

David is sad

Here is David in his camp.
(Hold up forefinger to be David.)
All his men are with him.
(Wave other fingers on that hand.)
A messenger comes running in,
(Mime running.)
Falls at David's feet.
(Bow at waist.)
David asks him, 'What's the news?'
(Spread hands with palms up.)
Told Saul and Jonathan are dead.
(Shake head.)

Here is David, very sad,
(Hold up finger and assume sad expression.)
Heard that his best friend is dead.
(Shake head sadly.)
Then he starts remembering
(Finger to head.)
All the happy times they had.
(Smile.)
David puts them in a song
(Mime playing instrument.)
To celebrate his friends.
(Shake hands.)

Joy Chalke

2 Samuel 1

A finger rhyme with actions to help tell the story.

If you know who David is

If you know who David is – clap your hands!
If you know who David is – clap your hands!

Bible people

33

Bible people

Let's all clap hands!

God chose him to be the king, a
surprise that made him sing,
If you know who David is – clap your
hands!

If you know who David is – shake your
fist!
If you know who David is – shake your
fist!
A shepherd very brave but small, he
made Goliath fall,
If you know who David is – shake your
fist!

If you know who David is – hide your
face!
If you know who David is – hide your
face!
He talks to God when he is scared and
he knows that he has heard,
If you know who David is – hide your
face!

If you know who David is – dry your
tears!
If you know who David is – dry your
tears!
God is near when he feels sad so things
don't seem quite so bad,
If you know who David is – dry your
tears!

If you know who David is – clap your
hands!
If you know who David is – clap your
hands!
A happy king who longs to give so his
name will always live,
If you know who David is – clap your
hands!

Sheila Clift

1 Samuel 16:1-13; 17; 19:11-12; 20;
23:14-18; 2 Samuel 1;7

♪ If you're happy and you know it

❗ This song examines several incidents in
David's life; choose verses as appropriate or
use the whole song to see how God was with
David in every situation.

I will miss them

Saul and Jonathan, Saul and Jonathan,
Strong as lions, strong as lions,
Fast as eagles, fast as eagles,
I will miss them, I will miss them.
How I loved them, how I loved them,
It was easy, it was easy.
I'm so sad now, I'm so sad now,
I will miss them, I will miss them.

Pam Macnaughton

2 Samuel 1

♪ London's Burning

❗ Sing as an echo song with a leader singing the
first phrase of each line, and everyone
repeating the words.

David and Nathan

King David said, 'I'm going to build
A temple wide and high,
(Open arms wide and stretch up.)
So God will know my love for him
Is bigger than the sky'.

But Nathan came with news from God.
He smiled and shook his head,
(Shake heads.)
'God does not want a temple.
Don't start to build,' he said.

'God knows how much you love him.
You do not need to prove,
And he will always care for you.
(Cross arms over chest.)
His love will never move.'

'Not because you're wise and good
Or for the things you do,
Not for gifts that you may give
(Stretch out arms.)
But just because you're you!'
(Cross arms on chest.)

- Sheila Clift
- 2 Samuel 7
- Row, row, row your boat
- An action song.

Solomon's wish

What happened to Solomon,
What happened to Solomon,
What happened to Solomon,
In Gibeon?

God spoke to Solomon,
God spoke to Solomon,
God spoke to Solomon,
In a dream.

What did God say,
What did God say,
What did God say,
To Solomon?

God made a promise,
God made a promise,
God made a promise,
To Solomon.

'I will do what you've asked,
I will do what you've asked,
I will do what you've asked,
King Solomon.'

What was the wish,
What was the wish,
What was the wish,
Of Solomon?

'I want to be wise,
I want to be wise,
I want to be wise,'
Said Solomon.

Did God keep his promise,
Did God keep his promise,
Did God keep his promise,
To Solomon?

Yes, God kept his promise,
Yes, God kept his promise,
Yes, God kept his promise,
To Solomon.

A very wise king,
A very wise king,
A very wise king,
Was Solomon.

- formerly in *Sing, say and move*
- 1 Kings 3:1–15; 2 Chronicles 1:1–13
- Divide group into two and say alternate verses; or a leader says verses in plain print and children say verses in italics; all join together for the last verse.

Solomon says

Solomon says, 'Do right.'
(Clap to one side.)
Solomon says, 'Love God.'
(Clap to the other side.)
Solomon says, 'God loves us so
(Clap up high.)
He will teach us and show us his way.'
(Turn round on the spot.)

- Maggie Barfield
- 1 Kings 3:1–15; 2 Chronicles 1:1–13; Proverbs 3, 4

Bible people

Let's all clap hands!

♪ Here we go Looby-lou

◇ An action song. Sing the song once, then mime or demonstrate a way in which we can do what 'Solomon says' which will help us to be wise and live God's way. Repeat song and mime several times, using a different way each time.

On the mountain

Elijah went up the mountain,
Elijah went up the mountain,
Elijah went up the mountain,
To find a place to hide.

But where could he find to hide?
But where could he find to hide?

He found a cave up the mountain,
He found a cave up the mountain,
He found a cave up the mountain,
And crept inside to hide.

God called to him on the mountain,
God called to him on the mountain,
God called to him on the mountain,
'Elijah, come outside.'

Elijah could not hide,
Elijah could not hide.

He talked to God on the mountain,
He talked to God on the mountain,
He talked to God on the mountain,
Out on the mountain side.

Maggie Barfield

1 Kings 19:8–18

♪ The bear went over the mountain

◇ 'Walk' your fingers up the 'mountain' of your other arm.

Naaman in the river

Down and up! That makes one!
This muddy river is no fun.

Down and up! That makes two!
This is a silly thing to do.

Down and up! That makes three!
I've still got spots all over me.

Down and up! That makes four!
My arms and legs and face are sore.

Down and up! That makes five!
Only two more times to dive.

Down and up! That makes six!
These nasty itchy spots still itch.

Down and up! One last time!
Hooray! Hooray! I'm feeling fine.

Maggie Barfield

2 Kings 5:1–19

◇ A counting rhyme; start standing up straight and then bob down and up in each verse.

Good (not really!) reasons for not using rhymes and songs with children

'Help - I can't sing!'

Most of us feel this way! But it really doesn't matter – sing anyway! Music is a way of making everyone feel involved. The pleasure is in sharing the song not musical perfection.

'And I can't play an instrument.'

To lead effectively, you need to be able to give the children your full attention, using your eyes, ears, hands and voice. Even good musicians may find it hard to lead as well as play! You could try:

- Asking a musician to come and play while you lead.
- Singing without musical accompaniment.
- Asking a musical friend to prepare a tape of music.
- Using a pre-recorded cassette tape of worship songs; many of these have words and music on one side and music only on the other.
- Having music playing at the beginning of the session to set the mood for the day.

'And I haven't got any musicians!'

Yes you have! Everyone in your group can be a musician! Children love to play with instruments, creating sound patterns and experimenting with rhythms. Try percussion instruments (to make your own, see pages 69 and 77). You won't want to use them for every song - children can't play and do actions at the same time - but you could:

- Choose a few children each week to form your percussion band.
- Sing one or two songs which the children know really well so they can play and still sing the words.
- Play along to recorded songs and music (which could be recordings of your own group).

Remember accompaniment does not have to be noisy: even very young children can learn to play instruments softly and put them down when they are not being used.

'I don't know how to teach new songs.'

Don't introduce too many new songs at one time, particularly with young children. Let one song become established before trying another.

Learning by repeating line after line is often the preferred method but it is slow. Instead try:

- Having a recording of the song playing in the background; when you come to learn it you will find the children have already become familiar with the tune and possibly the words too.
- Having the leader(s) sing the song through while the children accompany with instruments.
- Choosing a song with a chorus: teach just the chorus; then have leader(s) singing the verse and everyone singing the chorus.
- Singing a song several times so parts of lines are picked up and all can join in some of the song.
- Using songs and rhymes with lines or phrases which are repeated frequently.
- Using flip charts, flash cards or acetates to prompt.
- Using an illustrated version of song for non-readers, with key words or concepts replaced with a picture or symbol.
- Singing new words to a well-known tune so only part of the song is new.
- Choral rhymes, with everyone joining in a repeated line or phrase after each line read by a leader.

'The children in my group are too young to read.'

Participating helps children understand and remember the songs and rhymes. Actions, clapping and playing instruments all help the children to be involved in worship – whether they are singing or reading words or not. Worship is caught not taught. Children may not understand all the words and concepts but can sense the atmosphere. And they sometimes understand more than we give them credit for!

'I don't know what songs to sing.'

Build a repertoire of tried and tested songs. Don't be afraid to sing the same songs over and over, week after week. Children love repetition. It reassures them and helps them to learn.

Choose a 'theme tune' which you sing at the beginning or end of the session. It will help children develop a group identity and give them a secure routine.

Think about the mood and whether the mood of the tune matches the words. Children enjoy bright cheerful songs but it's sometimes good to have some quieter ones.

Let's all clap hands!

Elisha

Elisha was walking through Shunem one day,
(Walk on the spot.)
Out came a lady who stopped him to say,
(Hold up hand.)
'Come to our house and have something to eat,
(Beckon; mime eating.)
Come and sit down and rest your feet.'
(Indicate a chair.)

Elisha passed often and always came in,
(Wave.)
Said the lady, 'I want to do something for him.'
She had an idea and her husband agreed.
(Look pleased; nod.)
They built him a room which they thought he would need.
(Make a square shape with arms stretched.)

What did it have in it? What was in there?
A table and lamp, a bed and a chair.
(Make the shapes with your hands.)
Elisha saw this when he came to their home,
(Look surprised.)
And said, 'Thank you,' for all that the lady had done.

- Formerly in *Sing, say and move*
- 2 Kings 4:8–13
- An action rhyme.

The potter's house

Down at the potter's early in the morning,
See the little clay pots all in a row.
Along comes the potter, sits down at his wheel,
Picks up some fresh clay and off he goes!

- Maggie Barfield
- Jeremiah 18:1–17
- Down at the station
- A descriptive song to help children visualise what Jeremiah saw when he visited the potter; could also link to other stories like making pots for the temple, Isaiah's prophecies and imagery from Romans.

Jeremiah and the potter

Jeremiah watched the potter take a lump of clay.
Roll it, squash it, make it smooth, make a ball of clay.
And Jeremiah said, 'That's what God is like!'

Jeremiah watched the potter take that ball of clay,
Press it, stretch it, pull it upwards, make a little pot.
And Jeremiah said, 'That's what God is like!'

Jeremiah watched the potter as the pot went wrong.
Squash it, roll it, smooth it over, make a ball again.
And Jeremiah said, 'That's what God is like!'

Jeremiah watched the potter make the pot again.
Press it, stretch it, pull it upwards, make another pot.
And Jeremiah said, 'That's what God is like!'

Jeremiah watched the potter finishing his pot,
Flat base, nice shape and pretty pattern; what a useful pot!
And Jeremiah said, 'That's what God is like!'

Jeremiah watched the potter and God spoke to him.
'Like the potter, kind and gentle, I can shape your life.'
And Jeremiah said, 'That's what God is like!'

- Geraldine Witcher
- Jeremiah 18:1-17
- The rhyme explains what Jeremiah understood when he watched an everyday occurrence, and how he was able to use this to give God's message to the people.

Jeremiah in the well

Jeremiah told the people just what God had said: *(Point to one another.)*
'If you fight the enemy you're sure to end up dead.' *(Make fists.)*
Four men told the king, *(Four steps, then bow.)*
'Jeremiah must be stopped.
He's telling people not to fight.
He tells them there's no hope. *(Shake finger.)*
You must stop Jeremiah.'
The king said, 'Well, okay. *(Shrug, lift hands.)*
Do just what you like with him.'
And then he walked away. *(Walk a few steps.)*

They put Jeremiah down a well, *(Push down.)*
With thick and oozy mud.
But Ebedmelech told the king, *(Raise hand.)*
'What they've done is not good.
Poor Jeremiah's done no wrong. *(Shake finger.)*
You shouldn't treat him so.
He'll starve to death.' *(Pat tummy.)*
'All right,' the king said, 'you can let him go.' *(Raise hands.)*
Thirty soldiers pulled him out, with rags to save his skin. *(Pull.)*
Now Jeremiah's free at last, to speak God's word again. *(Finger to mouth.)*

- Margaret Spivey
- Jeremiah 38:1-13
- An action rhyme. For younger children, all do the actions as suggested. With older groups, this rhyme could be the basis for a drama.

Jonah

Jonah went to Nineveh
To tell everyone
They had made God unhappy
With the bad things they'd done.
Then everyone said sorry
And they cried and they prayed.
God was pleased and forgave them
And their city was saved!

- Maggie Barfield
- Jonah 1:1 – 3:10
- Away in a manger
- A simple song which stresses God's forgiveness when people repent

Bible people

Bible people

Let's all clap hands!

Jeremiah and the scroll

'I've a message to give you, Jeremiah, Jeremiah.
I've a message to give you, Jeremiah,' said God.

'Please help write it down, dear Baruch, dear Baruch.
Please help me write down this message from God.

Now please tell the king, dear Baruch, dear Baruch.
Now please give the king this message from God.'

**'But the king doesn't like it, Jeremiah, Jeremiah.
The king doesn't like the message from God.**

**He's cut up and burnt it, Jeremiah, Jeremiah.
The king has destroyed the message from God.'**

'God says start again, dear Baruch, dear Baruch.
We'll write down again the message from God.

And this time he'll listen, dear Baruch, dear Baruch.
This time the king will get the message from God.'

- Kathleen Crawford
- Jeremiah 36
- There's a hole in my bucket
- This story song could be sung by three voices or three groups.

Go, go Jonah!

Go, go, Jonah, (*Point.*)
To Nineveh!
Go, go, Jonah!
God wants you there!

Oh, oh, Jonah, (*Shake head.*)
Don't run away!
Oh, oh, Jonah!
There's trouble on the way.

Pray, pray, Jonah, (*Clasp hands together.*)
From inside the fish!
Pray, pray, Jonah!
God will hear your wish.

Up, up, Jonah, (*Move hands upwards.*)
Back on to dry ground!
Up, up, Jonah!
Spread the message round.

Off goes Jonah! (*Clap quickly.*)
The message has been sent!
And all the people
Knew what God meant!

- Elizabeth Alty
- Jonah 1:1 – 3:10
- Speak rhyme in a staccato rhythm.

Our friend Jesus

Day and night

Every day when I wake up,
Jesus, you're with me; you're always with me.
While I work and while I play,
Jesus, you're with me; you're always with me.
Jumping, running, helping, talking,
Jesus, you're with me; you're always with me.
You're right there beside me, day after day.
Jesus, you're with me; you're always with me.

Every night when I'm so sleepy,
Jesus, you're with me; you're always with me.
When I close my eyes up tight,
Jesus, you're with me; you're always with me.
Sleeping, dreaming, safe and cosy,
Jesus, you're with me; you're always with me.
You're right there beside me, night after night.
Jesus, you're with me; you're always with me.

- Christine Wright
- Matthew 28:20
- A responsive rhyme or prayer to affirm the presence of Jesus with us.

God is good

Jesus Christ knows the best way to live,
He has shown us his rules in the Bible.
We must love God with all of our hearts,
And our neighbour as ourselves.

Jesus, help us to follow your rules,
Help us to love God and think of other people.
Then at home, or at school, or at play,
We'll have fun as we care for one another.

- Sue Dunn
- Deuteronomy 28:1–14
- 'Stars and stripes' march by Sousa
- A rhyme to remind us how God wants us to live and a prayer to ask for his help to do so.

Jesus is light

Jesus is the light, shining oh so bright,
Jesus is the light, shining oh so bright,
Jesus is the light, shining oh so bright
Shining bright, shining bright, he's the light!

This little light of mine, I'm going to let it shine
This little light of mine, I'm going to let it shine
This little light of mine, I'm going to let it shine
Let it shine, let it shine, let it shine.

'Cos Jesus shines through me, Jesus shines through me,
Jesus shines through me, Jesus shines through me,
Jesus shines through me, Jesus shines through me,
Jesus shines, Jesus shines, shines through me!

- Angela Thompson

Our friend Jesus

Let's all clap hands!

- Luke 11:33-36
- This little light of mine
- Stand still in a circle and use arms to illustrate the words: 'Jesus is the light' - arms point up; 'shining oh so bright' - arms out sideways; 'shines through me' - touch shoulders, open arms wide.

Follow him

Follow him,
Only King,
Lord of every
Living thing.
Only Son of God is He.
Who can this great Saviour be?
He is Jesus! Give him Praise!
I will follow him all
My days!

- Rose Williams
- John 21:1-19
- An acrostic poem with a hidden message (first letter of each line).

Jump and sing

I feel like dancing, *(Pretend to dance.)*
Shouting and singing too,
(Punch the air on the word 'shout'.)
Learn to sing about Jesus, *(Hold out hands in front of you.)*
And you will feel it too.
(Point to the front.)
Swing like a monkey,
(Swing arms in front of body.)
Jump like a kangaroo, *(Jump.)*
Step and clap for Jesus,
(Step forward and clap.)
Because he loves me and you! *(Point to yourself and then to the front.)*

- Isabelle Irwin-Parker

- Acts 3:1-10; Psalms 98, 149, 150
- Use your bodies to celebrate and praise Jesus with this action rhyme.

Jesus is always with me

Jesus is with me in the park,
Jesus is there when it's getting dark.
Jesus is always with me!

Jesus is there when I'm in the car,
At playgroup, or eating a chocolate bar.
Jesus is always with me!

Jesus is there when I scrape my knees,
When I'm reading a book or climbing trees.
Jesus is always with me!

- Helen Burn
- Matthew 28:16-20
- A responsive prayer to affirm Jesus is with us all the time; improvise further verses using ideas from the children in your group.

I know

I cannot see the wind
When I look into the sky
But when I hear the rattling bins
I know the wind goes by.

Jesus is always near
To love me and to care.
I cannot see him by my side
But I know he's always there.

- Malc' Halliday
- We can't always see things but we know they exist. Could be used with themes about knowing Jesus is with us and at Pentecost.

Jesus loves us

Clap your hands for Jesus loves us;
Clap your hands for Jesus loves us;
Clap your hands for Jesus loves us;
What good news this is!

Wave your arms for Jesus loves us;
Wave your arms for Jesus loves us;
Wave your arms for Jesus loves us;
What good news this is!

Jump for joy for Jesus loves us;
Jump for joy for Jesus loves us;
Jump for joy for Jesus loves us;
What good news this is!

- Jacquie Sibley
- 'Bobby Shaftoe' and improvise some actions
- Use your bodies to celebrate the good news of Jesus

Listen to the news

Will you listen, will you listen?
To my news, to my news?
I know Jesus loves me. I know Jesus loves me.
Sing hooray! Sing hooray!

(Two skip around inside the circle as others clap and sing:)
(S)He has listened, he has listened
To the news, to the news.
He knows Jesus loves him, he knows Jesus loves him.
Sing hooray! Sing hooray!

(These two children then face two others and the song and actions are repeated. Change the second verse to:)
They have listened, they have listened,
To the news, to the news.
They know Jesus loves them, they know Jesus loves them.
Sing hooray! Sing hooray!

- Jacquie Sibley
- Acts 16:22–40
- Frère Jacques
- Explain that you're going to play a game about telling others the good news of Jesus' love for us. Sit in a circle with one child in the middle; that child faces another and pretends to share good news with him. All sing (to the tune of 'Frère Jacques').

  If you have a large enough group and sufficient space for eight children to skip inside your circle, repeat the song and actions a third time. With a smaller group, the four children could rejoin the circle and another child could stand in the middle as the game begins again.

You're there!

Jesus, when we go to playgroup
Thank you that you are always there.
Jesus, when we go to the shops
Thank you that you are always there.
Jesus, when we go to the park
Thank you that you are always there.
Jesus, when we play with our friends
Thank you that you are always there.

- Malc' Halliday
- A responsive prayer affirming Jesus is with us wherever we are.

Good news

Thank you, God for your good news
To share with everyone.
Jesus loves and cares for us,
He is your dear son.

- Jacquie Sibley
- Acts 16:22–40
- General application for stories about Jesus.

Our friend Jesus

Let's all clap hands!

Christmas

A baby for Elizabeth

Elizabeth was very sad, very sad, very sad.
Elizabeth was very sad, she longed for a baby.

Zechariah prayed to God, prayed to God, prayed to God.
Zechariah prayed to God, he longed for a baby.

The angel came with special news, special news, special news.
The angel came with special news, they would have a baby.

Zechariah couldn't speak, couldn't speak, couldn't speak.
Zechariah couldn't speak, till they'd had their baby.

Baby John was born to them, born to them, born to them.
Baby John was born to them, God's special messenger.

Everyone was happy then, happy then, happy then.
Everyone was happy then, thank you God!

- Joy Knott
- Luke 1:5–25
- Mary had a little lamb
- Choose children to be Zechariah, Elizabeth, and the angel. Ask them to stand in the centre of the circle while you practise the song again. Encourage 'Elizabeth' to be 'sad', 'Zechariah' to 'pray', and 'the angel' to 'stand like an angel'. Give Elizabeth the doll at the end.

Mary's song

I'm singing about how wonderful God is.
He's done wonderful things,
Special things for me that everyone will know about and praise him for.
He goes on loving us for year after year, for ever.
He does wonderful things.
Proud people have to bow down to him, but he lifts up the little ones.
He gives us good things to eat when we are hungry.
He's looking after his people just as he promised,
Just as he said he would.

- Geraldine Witcher
- Luke 1:26–56
- A version of Mary's song, the Magnificat, for young children.

An angel came

An angel came to Mary,
An angel came to Mary,
An angel came to Mary,
To bring her good news.

'Good tidings I bring
Of a new baby king.'
An angel came to Mary
To bring her good news.

- Helen Burn
- Luke 1:26–45
- A simple way to learn the angel's message.

Ahab was a greedy, greedy king

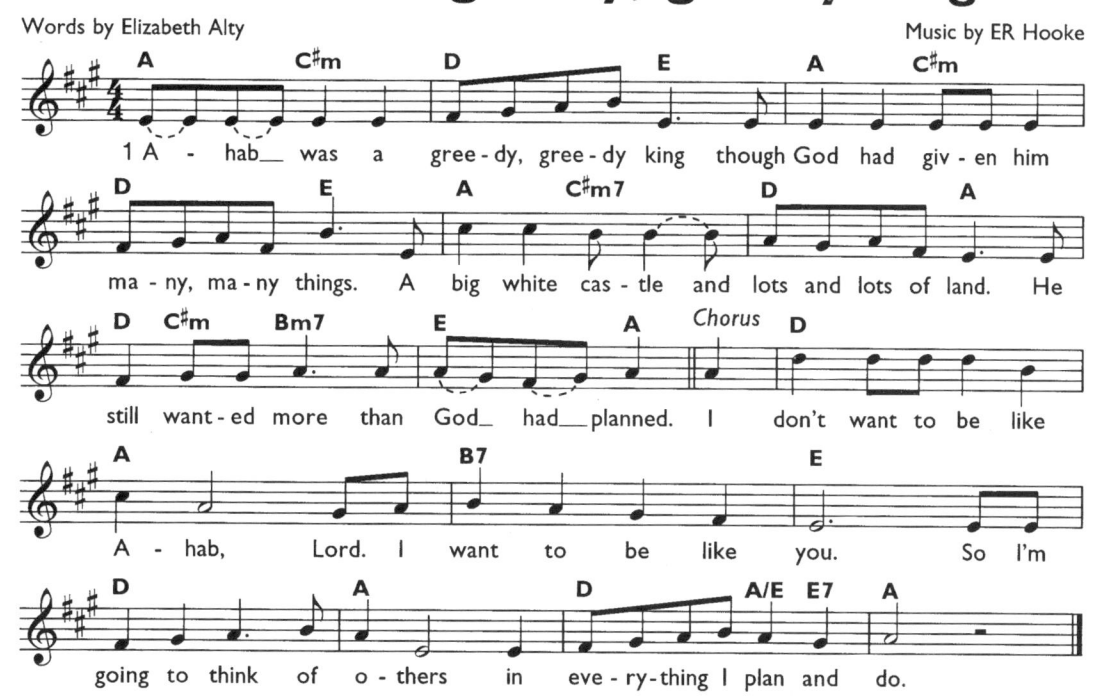

Words by Elizabeth Alty
Music by ER Hooke

1. Ahab was a greedy, greedy king though God had given him many, many things. A big white castle and lots and lots of land. He still wanted more than God had planned. *(Chorus)* I don't want to be like Ahab, Lord. I want to be like you. So I'm going to think of others in everything I plan and do.

2. Ahab wanted things so very, very bad.
   If he didn't get them he went oh so mad.
   I'll stamp my feet, I'll go straight off to bed
   I want my own way is what he always said.
   (Repeat chorus.)

© 1995 Scripture Union

Jesus the best friend

Words by Jacquie Sibley
Music by EM Stephenson

1. Jesus is the best friend, I know that he loves me. He helps me when I'm feeling sad, I'm glad that he loves me.

2. Jesus is the best friend,
   I know that he loves me.
   He helps me when I've done wrong things,
   I'm glad that he loves me.

3. Jesus is the best friend,
   I know that he loves me.
   He helps me when I feel alone,
   I'm glad that he loves me.

4. Jesus is the best friend,
   I know that he loves me.
   He helps me when I'm happy too,
   I'm glad that he loves me.

© Scripture Union 1970

Let's all clap hands

Let's all clap hands!

The angels' song

We love to sing, *(Hands on heart, then on either side of mouth.)*
Of God's great glory. *(Wiggle fingertips in a large arc.)*
We love to sing, *(Hands on heart, then on either side of mouth.)*
Of God's good news. *(Clap.)*

Don't be afraid, *(Cover, then uncover eyes with hands.)*
For God so loves you. *(Hands on heart.)*
Listen to us, *(Cup hand to ear.)*
We've got good news. *(Clap.)*

A baby is born, *(Rock arms.)*
He's come to help us. *(Shake hands with yourself.)*
A baby is born, *(Rock arms.)*
It's such good news. *(Clap.)*

Glory to God! *(Raise hands while waving.)*
And peace to his people! *(Palms together.)*
Glory to God! *(Raise hands while waving.)*
It's such good news! *(Clap.)*

Mary Houlgate
Luke 2:8–21
an action rhyme version of the song of the angels.

Shepherds on the hill

Here are the sheep, asleep on the hill
(Hand raised, fingers curled in.)
Here are the shepherds, watching them still.
(Wiggle two longest fingers of other hand.)
Bright angels came shining to send the good news,
(Wiggle all your fingertips quickly in the air.)
'A baby is born for me and for you.'
(Rock a baby; point to self and others.)
Dear Father, at Christmas, with presents and fun,
(Hands together; then spin hands in a circle.)
We thank you for your gift of your own precious son.
(Extend hands; then rock baby.)

Mary Houlgate
Luke 2:8–21
A finger rhyme.

Camel ride

Lollopy, lollopy, off we go,
The camel sways you to and fro.
Out in the desert three wise men
Travelled far to Bethlehem.

Lollopy, lollopy, off we go,
The camel sways you to and fro.
They rode on camels, followed a star,
To find the babe they travelled so far.

Lollopy, lollopy, off we go,
The camel sways you to and fro.
After many nights and many days
They found God's baby – shout 'Hooray!'
Hooray!

Susie Matheson
Matthew 2:1–12
Sway and amble along like laden camels!

Christmas animals

What did the donkey see?
Mary and Joseph trudging along.
Bethlehem's so far away.
Up and down hills and along dusty roads,
And will there be somewhere to stay?

What did the oxen see?
There in their manger, is Jesus asleep,
Small and special – a new baby boy!
And Mary and Joseph give great thanks to God
As they look at the baby with joy.

What did the sheep see?
The shepherds are minding them out on the hills
Keeping watch in the dark of the night,
When angels appear saying, 'Jesus is born',
And praising God in a bright light.

What did the camels see?
Far from the east come the clever wise men
And with them their presents they bring.
They follow a star as it shines in the sky
To find baby Jesus the king.

- Marjory Francis
- Christmas nativity stories

Far away

Far away and far away,
Looking at the starry skies,
Suddenly some wise men have
A big surprise!

One bright star appears and then
Seems to move across the skies.
So they start their journey to
Their big surprise!

On and on the wise men go,
Staring at the starry skies,
Till they find and kneel before
Their big surprise!

See the wise men travel home!
Smiling faces, happy eyes!
Now they know that Jesus is
God's big surprise!

- Formerly in *Let's join in!*
- Matthew 2:1-12
- Move around the room as you say this rhyme, pretending to be the wise men on their journey.

Great wise men

Great wise men lived in the east.
God sent a star so bright
To call the men to Bethlehem
And guide them by its light.

Great wise men set out at once,
Prepared to travel far.
With gold and perfumes rare and old,
They followed the bright star.

Great wise men reached Bethlehem,
They found a baby boy,
Lord Jesus sent to fill the world
With hope and love and joy.

- Formerly in *Let's Join in!*
- Matthew 2:1-12
- Walk round the room as you read the rhyme, following an imaginary or model star.

Let's all clap hands!

Look up!

Look up, look up, see the star
Shining on Bethlehem so far.
Ride, ride, follow the light
Through the day and through the night.

Bow, bow to the family
And Jesus on his mother's knee.
Give our gifts to the Prince of Love
Wave thank you to the star above.

- Formerly in *Let's Join in!*
- Matthew 2:1-12
- Improvise actions – look up, ride, bow, give.

Star so bright

Twinkle, twinkle, star so bright,
Twinkle, twinkle in the night,
Up above the world so high,
Wise men saw you in the sky.
Twinkle, twinkle, star so bright,
Twinkle, twinkle in the night.

Twinkle, twinkle, star so bright,
Twinkle, twinkle in the night,
God sent you to show the way,
To the house where Jesus lay,
Twinkle, twinkle, star so bright,
Twinkle, twinkle in the night.

- Formerly in *Sing, say and move*
- Matthew 2:1-12
- Twinkle, twinkle little star
- Open and shut fingers to twinkle like stars in the sky.

Wise men worship

Some wise men one night saw a very bright star,
Very bright star, very bright star,
Some wise men one night saw a very bright star
And knew that a King had been born.

Those wise men decided to follow the star…
To find the wonderful King.

King Herod was angry, but said with a smile,
Said with a smile, said with a smile,
'To Bethlehem go now and look for the child
And tell me when you have found him.'

The wise men looked everywhere in Bethlehem…
Until at last they found him.

They fell down and worshipped the Lord Jesus Christ,
Lord Jesus Christ, Lord Jesus Christ,
They gave him the presents they'd carried so far,
Frankincense, gold and myrrh.

And then the wise men travelled secretly home…
And so the Lord Jesus was safe.

- Formerly in *Sing, say and move*
- Matthew 2:1-12
- 'Here we go round the mulberry bush'
- A story rhyme game which tells the whole journey of the wise men; improvise simple actions to go with each verse.

Jesus' life

Four busy fishermen

Four busy fishermen,
Working by the sea.
Jesus came and called them,
'Come and follow me.'
Simon and Andrew came,
As quickly as could be,
So there were –
Two busy fishermen,
Working by the sea.

Two busy fishermen,
Working by the sea.
Jesus came and called them,
'Come and follow me.'
John and James came,
To see what they could see,
So there were –
Four following Jesus,
As happy as could be.

No busy fishermen,
Working by the sea,
But Jesus is still calling,
'Come and follow me.'
He wants us all to come along.
And that means you and me.
So come on –
Let's all follow Jesus,
As happy as can be.

- Maggie Barfield
- Matthew 4:18–22; Mark 1:16–20; Luke 5:1–11
- Five little bears bouncing on the bed
- As a counting rhyme or song; use fingers or models to help the counting and pause as appropriate to ask 'How many does that make?'

'Come and follow me'

Jesus went to Galilee
And rowed out on the sea, sea, sea.
He said 'Let down your net, net, net,
And see what you will get, get, get.'

The fishermen had a fright, fright, fright.
They pulled with all their might, might, might.
They heard a great big swish, swish, swish
And up came all the fish, fish, fish.

The nets began to rip, rip, rip,
And the boats began to tip, tip, tip.
They rowed back to the land, land, land,
And left them on the sand, sand, sand.

Jesus said 'Don't fear, fear, fear.
I always want you near, near, near,
So leave your nets by the sea, sea, sea,
And come and follow me, me, me.'

- Sheila Clift
- Matthew 4:18–22; Mark 1:16–20; Luke 5:1–11
- A sailor went to sea, sea, sea
- When you are familiar with the song, add three claps on the repeated words at the end of each line.

'Follow me!'

Jesus said 'Follow me, follow, follow me,
Over land and over sea, follow, follow me.
You can help me every day, follow, follow me,
So always listen when I say, follow, follow me.

Jesus' life

Let's all clap hands!

Sheila Clift
Matthew 4:18–22; Mark 1:16–20; Luke 5:1–11
Row row row your boat
Originally based on Jesus calling the fishermen but this rhyme or simple song could be linked with many stories when Jesus gives the challenge to people to follow him.

Row your boat

Row, row, row your boat
Strongly out to sea,
Drop your net and catch some fish
And bring them home for tea.

Throw, throw, throw your net
Out across the lake,
Catch a shiny silver fish
And bring it home to bake.

Maggie Barfield
Stories of Jesus and the fishermen
Row your boat
The song illustrates two methods of fishing used in Galilee. Sit on the floor one behind another and 'row' out to sea, or stand in the shallow water and cast out a net.

Early in the morning

Early in the morning, when really it's still night,
Jesus gets up quickly, before the sun is bright.
He needs to find a quiet place where he can think and pray:
He wants to ask his Father, God, to help him through the day.

Later in the morning when the sun is shining bright,
Jesus' sleepy friends wake up - they've slept right through the night.
They search for Jesus all around - wherever can he be?
'Let's go down to the beach,' says one, 'perhaps he's by the sea.'
When at last they find him, they ask, 'Lord, did you know
Everybody's looking for you? - Where did you go?'
'I was talking to my Father, God: I need his help today
So I asked him to show me who to help and what to say.

Christine Orme
Mark 1:35–39; Luke 4:42–44
A story in rhyme; say the first verse quietly to give the atmosphere of early morning.

Jesus heals

(Choose two children to stand in the centre of a circle, one to be 'Jesus' and the other to be, someone who is ill.)
This [girl] had a poorly head,
A poorly head, a poorly head.
This [girl] had a poorly head,
But Jesus made her well.' *('Jesus' touches the girl.)*

(All stand still and clap as the two children in the centre link hands and swing round. Sing:)
'Thank you Jesus, thank you now,
Thank you now, thank you now,
Thank you Jesus, thank you now
That you made this [girl] well.'

(All stand still and shout:)
Jesus is loving!
Jesus is powerful!
Jesus shows us what God is like!

Marjory Francis
Matthew 4:23–25; 8:16–18; Mark 1:32–39; Luke 4:40–44

♪ Here we go round the mulberry bush
⚠ A story song and game giving examples of Jesus' general healing ministry.

A man with leprosy

This poor man was very sick,
(Walk round looking sad.)
So he ran to Jesus, quick, quick, quick!
(Run, then stand still.)
Now this is the wonderful news we tell, *(Hold up a forefinger.)*
Jesus touched him, *(Pat arms.)* and now he's well! *(Clap and jump.)*

📖 Margaret Spivey
📕 Matthew 8:1-4; Mark 1:40-45; Luke 5:12-16
⚠ An action story rhyme

This poor man

(Children hug themselves, heads drooping.)
This poor man was very ill, very ill, very ill,
This poor man was very ill, very ill.

(Make 'shooing' movements.)
Everyone said, 'Go away, go away, go away,'
Everyone said, 'Go away, go away.'

(Hands outstretched, pleading.)
He asked Jesus, 'Make me well, make me well, make me well.'
He asked Jesus, 'Make me well.' Jesus touched him.

(Wave arms happily.)
Now he's telling everyone, everyone, everyone,
Now he's telling everyone, 'Jesus healed me!'

📖 Margaret Spivey
📕 Matthew 8:1-4; Mark 1:40-45; Luke 5:12-16
♪ London Bridge
⚠ An action story rhyme

Will you come?

(Roman)
Will you come and heal my slave?
I am a Roman!
Will you come and heal my slave?
For I am a Roman soldier.

(Jesus)
I will come without delay,
To help this Roman,
I will come without delay,
To help this Roman soldier.

(Roman)
No need to come to heal my slave,
Just give the order!
No need to come to heal my slave,
If Jesus gives the order!

(Jesus)
This Roman truly trusts in me,
He's very special,
This Roman truly trusts in me,
He really is very special!

(Roman)
Great! My slave is well again,
Hooray for Jesus!
Great! My slave is well again,
Hooray! Hooray for Jesus!

📖 Maggie Barfield
📕 Matthew 8:5-13; Luke 7:1-10
♪ We are the Romans
⚠ For two voices or two groups; each tells their own side of the story

Jesus' life

Let's all clap hands!

At Simon's house

See the lady, lying still. *(Right index finger horizontal.)*
She is feeling very ill.
Here is Jesus, wise and strong. *(Left index finger vertical.)*
Peter's glad he came along.
Jesus touched the lady's hand. *(Touch index fingers together.)*
At once she smiled, felt better and …
Got up! *(Raise right finger.)*
'I'm so much better now,' she said.
'I don't need to stay in bed.' *(Wiggle right finger.)*

Jacquie Sibley

Matthew 8:14,15; Mark 1:29-31; Luke 4:38,39

A finger rhyme

Jairus and Jesus

Jairus had a daughter who was sick, sick, sick,
So he ran to ask Jesus to be quick, quick, quick.
'I know you can make her better' Jairus said,
But on the way, they heard that she was dead, dead, dead.

Jesus went and stood beside her bed, bed, bed,
'Get up, little child,' was what he said, said, said.
Jairus' daughter opened up her eyes
And looked around at everyone in great surprise.

Maggie Barfield

Matthew 9:18-26; Mark 5:21-43; Luke 8:40-56

Miss Polly had a dolly

The content of the story is reflected in the well-known tune.

A daddy and his son

A daddy loved his son so much, son so much, son so much,
A daddy loved his son so much, in Jesus' time.

But one day the boy got sick, boy got sick, boy got sick,
But one day the boy got sick, they were worried!

His daddy went to ask Jesus, ask Jesus, ask Jesus,
His daddy went to ask Jesus to make him better.

Straight away the boy got well, boy got well, boy got well,
Straight away the boy got well, they were happy!

Then everybody loved Jesus, loved Jesus, loved Jesus,
Then everybody loved Jesus, they loved Jesus!

Angela Thompson

John 4:43-53

London Bridge

Improvise a dance to go with this song; or simply hold hands in a circle and walk round, changing direction after each verse.

52

On tiptoe

Words by Marjory Francis
Music by Kathryn Wright

1 Treading on tiptoe,
  We enter the gloom
  And the smell and the filth
  Of that small stable room.
  We gaze at the baby
  In rough manger bed,
  And rejoice in Emmanuel
  As on tiptoe we tread.

2 Standing on tiptoe,
  Our voices we raise.
  The Lord comes among us
  Enjoying our praise.
  We bathe in his presence,
  We feed from his hand,
  His Spirit unites us
  As on tiptoe we stand.

3 Gazing on tiptoe,
  Our hearts wait and yearn
  And remember his promise
  'I will surely return.'
  We long for his coming,
  When all will be praise.
  Yes, we look for the King
  As on tiptoe we gaze.

© Scripture Union

Jesus' life

Let's all clap hands!

The man who was deaf

Here is a man whose ears don't really work, *(Hold up right index finger for man, touch ears and shake head.)*
A lonely man who finds it hard to talk. *(Shrug shoulders; look down.)*
Here is a man who's frightened and sad, *(Shrinking gesture.)*
Here is a man who never feels glad. *(Outline down-turned mouth with finger.)*
Now Jesus beckons, saying, 'Come with me.' *(Beckon with left index finger.)*
Looks up to heaven, touching ears and tongue gently. *(Look up, touch ears and tongue.)*

Here is Jesus, making the man well, *(Hold up 'Jesus' finger again.)*
Saying to the people there, 'Please don't tell!' *(Finger on lips and shake head.)*
But here are the people who rush off to tell, *(Waggle all fingers.)*
What's happened to the deaf man they know so well. *(Make 'talking mouth' from fingers and thumb.)*
'Jesus is brilliant!' they all say, *(Thumbs up sign, big smiles.)*
'Just wait till you hear what he did today!' *(Hold hands up in astonishment, look amazed.)*

Here is the man whose ears **do** work! *(Hold up right finger, touch ears and nod vigorously.)*
A friendly man who loves to talk! *(Make 'talking mouth' with fingers and thumb.)*
Here is a man who's happy, not sad. *(Big smiles.)*
Here is the man that Jesus made glad!

Christine Orme
Mark 7:31–37
an action rhyme to show the feelings as well as the facts of this healing miracle

Helping and healing

Four hurt people live nearby,
Needing Jesus – that makes five!
One sick woman, hurt so much,
Healed by Jesus, with a touch.
One called Jairus, daughter sick,
'Rush for Jesus, quick, quick, quick!'
One sad mother, crying said,
'Go tell Jairus that she's dead.'
One girl lives when Jesus said,
'Get up now, child. Eat some bread.'
Four glad people pleased to say,
'Jesus cared for us today.'

Christine Wright
Matthew 9:18–26; Mark 5:21–43; Luke 8:40–56
A counting rhyme; use finger puppets to tell the story.

Our Father

Thank you Jesus for loving us,
Just like our Father in heaven.
Thank you, Jesus, for always being there,
Just like our Father in heaven.
Thank you Jesus for giving us all that we need.
Just like our Father in heaven.

Rose Williams
Matthew 14:13–21; Mark 6:30–44; Luke 9:10–27; John 6:1–14
A responsive prayer using Bible words

Bartimaeus

Here comes Bartimaeus,
Here comes Bartimaeus,
Here comes Bartimaeus,
He's blind, he cannot see.

He shouts out loud to Jesus,
He shouts out loud to Jesus,
He shouts out loud to Jesus,
'Please Jesus – make me see!'

Jesus stops and heals him,
Jesus stops and heals him,
Jesus stops and heals him,
And Jesus makes him see.

Here comes Bartimaeus,
Here comes Bartimaeus,
Here comes Bartimaeus,
As different as can be!

- Maggie Barfield
- Mark 10:46-52 (Luke 18:35-43 does not name the man)
- Round and round the village
- The repetitive pattern of this story song means children can pick up the words and join in easily.

Love

Here is Jesus. He tries to explain
God wants us to love him, again and again.
Here is a good man, wanting to know,
What does God really want? What must we do?

Jesus tells the man just what he should do:
First love God, then other people, too.
The man says, 'I'll love God with all of my might!'

So Jesus says 'Wonderful! You know that's right.'

- Margaret Spivey
- Exodus 20:1-7; Mark 12:28-34
- Retell the story for very young children, using two hand puppets, to show what God wants of people and how he wants us to live.

Feeding the five thousand

Five thousand people
Climbing up a hill
Wanting to hear Jesus
And to be made well.

'How can we feed them all?'
Said Jesus to his friends.
'They'll all be very hungry
Before today ends.'

'There's one small boy
Sitting over there,
He has a picnic lunch
Which we could share.'

Two small fishes and
Five loaves of bread –
The boy gave them to Jesus,
Five thousand were fed.

- formerly in *Sing, say and move*
- Matthew 14:13-21; Mark 6:30-44; Luke 9:10-17; John 6:1-14
- a rhyme story, including reference to the boy with the food (from John's gospel); could form the basis of a simple group drama

Jesus' life

Let's all clap hands!

Ten sick men

Ten sick men all walking in a line,
One saw Jesus, so did the other nine.

Ten men scared that Jesus wouldn't wait,
Two ran forward, so did the other eight.

Ten men thought being better would be heaven.
Three called, 'Jesus!' So did the other seven.

Ten men limping, leaning on their sticks.
Four saw Jesus stop! So did the other six.

Ten men didn't wait for Jesus to arrive.
Five called, 'Please help us!' So did the other five.

Ten men knocked on the synagogue door,
Six found the priest, so did the other four.

Ten men laughing, shouting, 'Look at me!'
Seven said, 'I'm well again!' So did the other three.

Ten men wondering, 'Now what shall we do?'
Eight said, 'I'm going home!' So did the other two.

Ten men leaping and dancing in the sun,
Nine ran into town, but not the other one.

One man remembered who had helped all ten, he ran back to Jesus, thanked him and then,
Jesus blessed him and sent him on his way, and that man was well from that very day.

Rose Williams
Luke 17:11-19
Use your fingers and thumbs to be the ten men in this rhyme – you'll need to be nimble-fingered to get the numbering correct!

Jesus shines!

Jesus, how lovely you are!
Your clothes are shining, you're bright as a star!
Jesus, there's light all around.
I'm so amazed, I daren't make a sound!

Elizabeth Alty
Matthew 17:1-8; Mark 9:2-8; Luke 9:28-36
A childlike response to an amazing event

Wake up!

Wake up! Jump up! *(Jump up.)*
Jesus is your friend! *(Point around.)*
Wake up! Jump up! *(Jump.)*
His love will never end! *(Hold hands in a circle.)*
But I'm so tired.... *(Lie down.)*
We wake up! We jump up! *(Jump up.)*
Jesus we do thank you! *(Clap.)*
We wake up! We jump up! *(Jump.)*
Because your words are true! *(Clap.)*
Hooray! *(Skip and dance.)*

Elizabeth Alty
Matthew 17:1-8; Mark 9:2-8; Luke 9:28-36
Follow the suggested actions and express your praise with your bodies.

Shine Jesus

Jesus took three friends up a big hill to pray. *(Walk.)*
All of them were tired, they'd had a busy day. *(Yawn.)*
The three tired friends fell fast asleep at prayer. *(Head on hands.)*
Jesus prayed alone. His father God was there. *(Raise hands.)*

When his friends awoke, they had a great surprise. *(Rub eyes.)*
Jesus looked so different, right before their eyes! *(Gasp.)*
Jesus was amazing. He stood there, all in white. *(Look surprised.)*
He talked with God his father, shining, shining bright. *(Spread arms wide.)*

The friends were all amazed. Peter said, 'What shall we do?'
God said, 'Listen to Jesus. All his words are true.' *(Cup ears.)*
When the light began to fade, the friends thought of what they'd heard. *(Look puzzled.)*
They came down from the mountain but they dare not speak a word. *(Finger on lips.)*

- Elizabeth Alty
- Matthew 17:1-8; Mark 9:2-8; Luke 9:28-36
- Try the suggested actions or mime/act out the rhyme to help children understand this amazing story.

Mary's gift

Mary had a special gift
Special gift, special gift
Mary had a special gift
A special gift for Jesus.

Mary gave her special gift
Special gift, special gift
Mary gave her special gift
She gave her love to Jesus.

Have you got a special gift?
Special gift, special gift?
Have you got a special gift?
A special gift for Jesus?

Let's all give a special gift
Special gift, special gift
Let's all give a special gift
Let's give our love to Jesus.

- Maggie Barfield
- Matthew 26:6-13; Mark 14:3-9; Luke 7:36-50; John 12:1-8 (not all these accounts name 'Mary')
- Mary had a little lamb
- Form two lines facing each other; dance towards and apart on alternate lines.

Jesus' life

Let's all clap hands!

Mountain top

Glorious mountain
High hill *(Make hill shape with hands high above head.)*
Steep way *(Make sharp inverted V-shape with hands.)*
Hard climb *(Wipe sweat from brow.)*
Special day.
(Make voice and face excited.)
Three friends sleep
(Head on folded hands, eyes closed.)
While Jesus prays. *(Hands together.)*
Two men walk
On mountain top
(Make two fingers of one hand 'walk'.)
Elijah and Moses: *(Raise one finger of right hand for each name.)*
Friends of God.
(Raise both hands in worship.)
Talk with Jesus,
(One finger on left hand 'talks' to two fingers on right hand.)
They know why *(Nod head wisely.)*
God's own Son
Has to die. *(Make sad face.)*
Peter wakes, *(Stretch and yawn.)*
Rubs his eyes, *(Rub eyes.)*
James and John! *(Whisper urgently.)*
Surprise! Surprise! *(Act startled.)*
Shimmering, shining *(Wiggle fingers.)*
Dazzling bright! *(Hold hands, palms outward, in front of shoulders.)*
Shaded eyes, *(Shade eyes.)*
Glorious light!
(Peer out from under hands.)
Who's with Jesus?
What's going on? *(Puzzled expression.)*
A special place *(Point with one hand.)*
A special day,
(Point up with other hand.)
Let's build three tents *(Make inverted U-shape with hands three times.)*
Where they can stay.
But three tents *(Make inverted U-shape with hands three times.)*
Are not God's plan; *(Shake head.)*
Misty cloud
(Wave hands gently in front of face.)
Hides the men.
(Bring hands in front of face.)
Heavenly voice *(Cup ear and look up.)*
Makes them stop.
'This is my chosen Son
You see;
Listen well
(Raise one finger in warning.)
He comes from me.'
Time to go *(Make fingers 'walk'.)*
Down and down
(Make fingers go down hill.)
Quietly thoughtful *(Put one finger to cheek in thoughtful pose.)*
Back to town. *(Make fingers 'walk'.)*

Beth McLean

Matthew 17:1-13; Mark 9:2-13; Luke 9: 28-36

The story of Jesus' transfiguration told in rhyme, with actions to help the children understand and become involved in the event.

Stories Jesus told

The sower

The farmer sowed his seeds,
The farmer sowed his seeds,
Left and right, all around,
The farmer sowed the seeds.

Some seeds fell on the path,
Some seeds fell on the path,
The birds flew down and ate them up,
Some seeds fell on the path.

Some seeds fell on the rocks,
Some seeds fell on the rocks,
The sun was much too hot for them,
Some seeds fell on the rocks.

Some seeds fell near the thorns,
Some seeds fell near the thorns,
The thorns were much too strong for them,
Some seeds fell near the thorns.

Some seeds fell in good soil,
Some seeds fell in good soil,
They grew up tall and strong and straight,
Some seeds fell in good soil.

- Christine Orme
- Matthew 13:1–9; Mark 4:1–9; Luke 8:4–15
- The farmer's in his den
- Choose one child to be the farmer while everyone else pretends to be the seeds; let the farmer mime sowing the seeds but when you come to the last verse, everyone runs into a space and mimes being a seed growing tall, strong and straight. Repeat with another child as 'farmer'.

Do it yourself

You don't put _____ in your bed!
You don't put _____ on your head!
You don't make a _____ and then sleep on it!
And you don't put a light where no one can see it!

You don't put _____ in the bath!
You don't leave _____ on the path!
You don't grow a _____ and then dance with it!
And you don't put a light where no one can see it!

You don't put _____ in the bin!
You don't put _____ in a tin!
You don't find _____ and then sing to it!
And you don't put a light where no one can see it!

You don't put _____ on the beach!
You don't find _____ inside a peach!
You don't _____ and then race with it!
And you don't put a light where no one can see it!

- Jonathan Gower
- Matthew 5:15; 6:22,23; Luke 11:33–36
- Show the children the first verse of the poem. Explain that it's about things just as silly as lighting a lamp and then putting it under a bowl or mixing up good and bad things. Work with the children to complete the poem. Any words will do, just make it sound as silly as possible! Enjoy your poem together. You could practise performing it or you could illustrate and display it.

Stories Jesus told

Let's all clap hands!

The lost son

There once was a hard-working father
Who worked on his farm with his sons.
But one son was fed up with working –
He wanted to have lots of fun.

He said, 'Dad, I want all my money.
I'm going to leave right away'
His father was sad, for he loved him,
And wished that his young son would stay.

The son went away to the city;
Had fine clothes and parties and friends
But nobody wanted to know him
When his money had come to an end.

He needed some help; he was hungry
But nobody wanted to know.
He got a job down on a pig farm –
There seemed nowhere else he could go.

'I'm going to go home to my father,'
The young man decided at last.
'I'll tell him that I'm very sorry.
He might give me a job if I ask.'

Now, back home, the father was waiting
(He'd been waiting and watching each day),
Longing and loving and hoping,
From the time that his son went away.

Then one day his long wait was over –
He saw a thin figure he knew!
He ran to his son and he hugged him!
The son hugged his father back, too!

What had happened before, didn't matter –
His dad was so glad he was there.
Called the servants to cook for a party
And bring his son new clothes to wear.

At the farm there was great celebration –
Such music and dancing around –
And the happiest man was the father
For his son who was lost, had been found!

Maggie Barfield

Luke 15:11–32

A rhyme version of one of Jesus' best-loved stories

The farmer and his field

The farmer had a big field.
He planted many seeds,
But one night came a bad man
And put in lots of weeds.

'Oh look!' the workers shouted,
When plants began to grow.
'Weeds growing in our wheat field,
There's some in every row!'

'Just leave the weeds to grow there,'
The clever farmer said,
'For if we try and pull them up
We might pick wheat instead.'

So when the wheat was ready:
A lovely golden-brown,
'It's harvest-time!' the farmer said,
'The wheat and weeds cut down.'

'Then take the wheat, it's good and sweet,
Into my barn to stay,
But put those bad weeds on the fire,
Until they burn away!'

Formerly in *Sing, say and move*

Matthew 13:24–30

Improvise mimed action.

Looking forward

Words by Dorothy Johnson

Music by Mrs JW Wood

1 Thank you God for things to do, for friends to play, for all who care.
Thank you God for days to share and for looking forward.

2 Thank you God for parks to play,
A bike to ride, a frame to climb.
Thank you God for sunny days
And for looking forward.

3 Thank you God for party times,
For birthday treats and Christmas fun.
Thank you God for special days
And for looking forward.

© Scripture Union

Sunday comes

Words by Elizabeth Alty

Music by Maggie Barfield

Monday comes, it's washing day. Tuesday comes, we jump and play. Wednesday comes, let's paint and draw. Thursday comes, let's sweep the floor. Friday comes, we bake all day. Saturday comes, we've friends to stay. BUT— When Sunday comes, we all race to get together at our meeting place!

Words © Elizabeth Alty
Music © Scripture Union

Let's all clap hands!

Let's all clap hands!

These are the seeds

These are the seeds the farmer sowed, *(Mime sowing seeds.)*
To grow into corn, *(Grow upwards.)*
To grind into flour,
(Pretend to grind and twist hands.)
To bake into bread, *(Knead dough.)*
For the farmer to eat for breakfast.
(Mime eating.)

These are the seeds the farmer sowed,
That fell on the path, *(Touch one palm with the fingers of the other.)*
Where there was no soil, *(Shake head.)*
So hungry birds swooped down,
(Waggle fingers.)
And ate them all for their breakfast.
(Make a beak with finger and thumb.)

These are the seeds the farmer sowed,
That fell near some stones, *(Make a fist.)*
Where the ground was hard,
(Gently knock two fists.)
So plants would not grow, *(Shake head.)*
To make bread for the farmer's breakfast.

These are the seeds that the farmer sowed,
Which grew near weeds that
(Wiggle fingers.)
Were prickly and big, *(Interlock fingers.)*
So plants would not grow, *(Shake head.)*
To make bread for the farmer's breakfast.

These are the seeds that the farmer sowed,
Which fell in good soil, *(Smile.)*
And grew strong and tall,
(Stretch up tall.)
So there was lots of flour
(Grind and twist.)
To make bread for the farmer's breakfast. *(Mime eating.)*

Kathleen Crawford
Matthew 13:1–9; Mark 4:1–9; Luke 8:4–15
An action story rhyme.

Little seeds

This little seed *(Hold up finger and thumb to show size.)*
Fell on the path. *(Point to the floor.)*
Someone trod on it, *(Stamp.)*
Then a bird ate it, *(Swooping action.)*
And that was that! *(Shrug shoulders.)*

This little seed *(Finger and thumb.)*
Fell near the rocks. *(Make fists.)*
Hard dry ground
(Make fists into hammers.)
Was such a shock, *(Shrink back.)*
So this little plant dried up! *(Shudder.)*

This little seed *(Finger and thumb.)*
Fell near the thorns. *(Scratching movements.)*
Prickly and cruel, *(Snarl.)*
They choked the seed, *(Wring hands.)*
So this little seed gave up!
(Shake head sadly.)

But **this** little seed
(Finger and thumb, smile.)
Fell on good ground *(Thumbs up.)*
Sent shoots **up!** *(Point upwards.)*
Sent roots **down!** *(Point down.)*
And grew tall and strong and straight!
(Put hands together and raise above head.)
Hooray! *(Clap.)*

Christine Orme
Matthew 13:1–9; Mark 4:1–9; Luke 8:4–15
A finger-and-hand rhyme.

Looking for the sheep

We're looking for the lost sheep.
We won't come home 'til we find him.
We might meet a lion.
We might meet a bear
But we're not scared.
God will take care of us.
Let's go.

Ah, ah. What's this?
It's long grass.
Can't go over it, can't go under it, can't go round it,
Have to go through it.
Let's go.

We're looking for the lost sheep ...

Ah, ah. What's this?
It's a river.
Can't go over it, can't go under it, can't go round it,
Have to swim through it.
Let's go.

We're looking for the lost sheep ...

Ah, ah. What's this?
It's a hill.
Can't go over it, can't go under it, can't go round it,
Have to climb up it.
Let's go.
And run down it.

We're looking for the lost sheep ...

Ah, ah. What's this?
It's some brambles.
Listen!
I can hear something.

It's a sheep!
Through the brambles.
Ow! They're prickly!
Here it is.
Hooray!
Let's go home.

Ah, ah. What's this?
It's big. It's furry.
It's got sharp teeth.
It's a lion!

Up the hill –
Down the hill –
Through the river –
Through the long grass –
And home.
God did take care of us.
Thank you, God.

Lynda Broadley

Matthew 18:12-14; Luke 15:4-7

Play this searching game like the traditional 'lion hunt' game.

Seeds

Seed can be long,
Seed can be round,
All sorts of seeds are in the ground.
(Stretch out, curl up, wiggle arms outstretched.)

A seed is small,
A seed grows tall,
Thank you, God, for them all.
(Starting crouched up on the floor and growing taller with each line, arms up at the end.)

Susanne and Mark Hopkins

Matthew 13:1-9; Mark 4:1-9; Luke 8:4-15

Pretend to be growing seeds with this action rhyme; use with parables of growth.

Stories Jesus told

Let's all clap hands!

Wise and careless builders

A wise man went to build a home E-I-E-I-O,
He built it well of bricks and stone E-I-E-I-O,
He built it strong, he built it tall,
That house would stand and would not fall,
A wise man went to build a home E-I-E-I-O.

A careless man began a home E-I-E-I-O,
He made it out of sand, not stone E-I-E-I-O,
He built it cheap, he built it fast,
But did not build his house to last,
A careless man began to build E-I-E-I-O.

And then the rain began to fall E-I-E-I-O,
The wise man hardly knew at all E-I-E-I-O,
His fine house kept the water out,
A good firm house, without a doubt,
The wise man's house stood strong and sure E-I-E-I-O.

The harsh wind blew, the rain lashed down E-I-E-I-O,
The careless man began to frown E-I-E-I-O,
The rain poured in through lots of leaks,
The roof began to sag and sink,
And then – oh no! – the house fell down! E-I-E-I-O.

- Maggie Barfield
- Matthew 7:24–29; Luke 6:47–49
- Old Macdonald had a farm
- Mime building (one fist on top of another), rain (fingers wiggling down), firm house (stand to attention), and fallen house (collapse on the floor).

The greatest treasure

One, two, three, four, five, (*Hold up fingers, one by one.*)
In a field, rich treasure find. (*Mime digging.*)
Six, seven, eight, nine, ten, (*Hold up fingers of other hand.*)
Cover it right up again. (*Mime covering.*)
'Why did you hide it, friend?' (*Raise finger questioningly.*)
'To own the treasure in the end.' (*Point to self.*)
Sing for Jesus every day, (*Hands on heart.*)
He's so special, shout 'Hooray!' (*Hands in air, jump and shout.*)

One, two, three, four, five, (*Hold up fingers, one by one.*)
See a shiny pearl so fine. (*Hand above eyes.*)
Six, seven, eight, nine, ten, (*Hold up fingers of other hand.*)
I want to see the pearl again. (*Hand above eyes again.*)
It's the pearl I long to own, (*Beckon.*)
It is such a precious stone. (*Hold out hands palms together.*)
Sing for Jesus every day, (*Hands on heart.*)
He's so special, shout 'Hooray!' (*Hands in air, jump and shout.*)

- Alison Irving
- Matthew 13: 44–46
- Once I caught a fish alive
- Tell one or both these stories Jesus told and emphasise that Jesus is the best treasure any of us could have.

Good neighbours?

This is Fred and this is Joe.
They're next-door neighbours, don't you know?
And one night, when they were both asleep
And there was no sound, not even a peep,
There was a knock at Joe's door …
And when he opened it, he saw – a friend!
Who'd come to see him again.

So Joe said, 'Hello, Friend,
You've come to see me again.
I can't believe it's true!
How are you?' And the friend said,
'Hello, Joe, I'm well you know
But I've come a long way and I need to be fed
So Joe, can I please have some bread?'

And Joe thought:
'Bread, bread, he's asked me for bread!
He needs some bread so he can be fed.'
'But,' Joe said, 'I haven't got any bread!'
'I know,' thought Joe, 'I'll go and ask Fred.'
So Joe knocked at Fred's door
And Joe said to Fred:
'Hey Fred, it's Joe you know.
I need some bread to give to my friend
My friend who's come to see me again.
So please Fred, can you give me some bread?'

And then Fred said:
'No, Joe, you'll have to go.
I'm in my bed, I can't give you bread,
Go Joe,' Fred said. So Joe said:
'But Fred, Fred, I need some bread.
I need some bread to give to my friend,
My friend who's come to see me again.
If I get no bread he won't get fed.
So, please Fred, get out of your bed.
Get out of your bed and give me some bread.
I need some bread, some bread, please Fred!'

And Fred said:
'Look Joe, you're right I know.
You need some bread to give to your friend,
Your friend who's come to see you again.
You need some bread, so he can get fed.
You need some bread, so you came to ask Fred.
Well, since you've asked, I'll get out of my bed,
I'll get out of my bed
AND I'LL GIVE YOU SOME BREAD!
I'll give you some bread, so your friend can be fed.
AND JOE,' Fred said, 'PLEASE GO
When you get the bread.'
So just 'cos Joe asked, Fred got out of his bed.
He left his bed to get some bread
And Joe and his friend they both got fed,
Got fed because Joe had asked for bread,
Got fed on the bread that had come from Fred.
So his friend and Joe, were happy you know.
And as for Fred,
HE WENT STRAIGHT BACK TO BED!

Jonathan Gower
Matthew 6:9-13; 7:7-11; Luke 11:1-8
Practise this story rhyme before you use it, to get the rhythm flowing well.

Easter

Let's all clap hands!

Easter

The donkey's first journey

Little donkey standing there
With your grey and shaggy hair,
In the heat and dusty air,
Haven't heard of Jesus.

Tied up to a wooden door,
No one sat on you before.
Saddle, reins, you never wore,
But you're there for Jesus.

Hear the sound of running feet –
Two men come along the street.
They the little donkey greet:
'We need you for Jesus.'

Taken off along the way
Little donkey does not bray
Though this is the strangest day.
Soon you will meet Jesus.

Ridden by the gentlest man
Little donkey finds he can
Be a part of God's big plan
And a help to Jesus.

With your King you walk on by,
See the branches waving high,
Hear the noise that fills the sky:
'Shout hooray for Jesus!'

Marjory Francis

Matthew 21:2-9; Mark 11:2-10; Luke 19:30-38

Re-enact the Palm Sunday procession, using this story rhyme.

Red ribbons

On Palm Sunday Jesus rode into Jerusalem on a donkey.
Everyone shouted 'Hosanna!'
(Dance, waving ribbons and shouting 'Hosanna!')
BUT…
(Wait until everyone is still.)
Jesus was taken away by soldiers and they made him carry his cross.
Everyone followed.
(Circle the room slowly; drag ribbons by one end, ending up at the cross.)
Jesus died on the cross for all the bad things we have done.
(Drape the ribbons over the arms of the cross so that they hang down. Stand quietly.)
(Spread out the cloth and carefully lift the ribbons down to lie on it, as you speak.)
When Jesus was dead, his friends took him down and wrapped him up and put him in a cave.
(Fold the cloth with the ribbons in it.)
But after three days, Jesus was alive! He had risen!
(Shake out the cloth and send the ribbons flying. Tell the children to each pick one up.)
Now we can be happy because Jesus is alive for ever.
(Let the children dance round again waving their ribbons shouting 'Jesus is risen!', 'Hooray', 'Hallelujah' etc.)

Rose Williams

Matthew 21-28; Mark 11:2-10; 14: 46; 15:20-47; 16:1-8; Luke 19:30-38; 22:47-54; 23:26-56; 24:1-33

A dramatic reconstruction of the Easter story. Needed: one metre of red ribbon for each person, a box to put them in, a cross, a piece of white cloth at least a metre square. Give each child a ribbon. Show them how to hold one end and wave it. As you tell the story, demonstrate the actions with the ribbons for the children to copy. Stand the cross nearby, with the cloth out of sight.

Jesus' journey

These are the olives that grew on the trees,
The trees that stood on the Mount of Olives near Jerusalem.
(Show the jar of olives.)

These are the friends whom Jesus sent,
To fetch the donkey for his strange journey,
From the Mount of Olives to Jerusalem.
(Show a picture of the disciples.)

This is the rope that the friends took,
To fetch the donkey that no one had ridden,
To take Jesus on his strange journey,
From the Mount of Olives to Jerusalem.
(Show the rope.)

This is the man who owned the donkey,
That no one had ridden,
That the friends went to fetch,
To take Jesus on his strange journey,
From the Mount of Olives to Jerusalem.
(Show the picture of the man.)

The friends told the man,
'We're here to fetch this donkey
Which no one has ridden,
To take Jesus on a journey,
From the Mount of Olives to Jerusalem.'
(Show the disciples again.)

These are the branches that people took,
To wave and shout 'Hosanna, hooray'
And 'Let us praise aloud today',
As Jesus came along the way,
On his journey,
From the Mount of Olives to Jerusalem.
(Show the branch.)

These are the clothes people threw on the way,
As they shouted 'Praise King Jesus today!'
As he came on his journey
From the Mount of Olives to Jerusalem.
(Show the jacket.)

These are the friends who felt very proud,
As they walked by the donkey and heard the crowd,
Praising King Jesus and shouting out loud,
'Hosanna, hooray: Praise Jesus today!'
As he came on his journey,
From the Mount of Olives to Jerusalem.
(Show the disciples again.)

Peggy Gibson/Marjory Francis

Matthew 21:2-9; Mark 11:2-10; Luke 19:30-38

You will need: a jar of olives, a piece of rope (skipping rope or washing-line), pictures of the disciples and the donkey's owner, a branch and a jacket.

Make sure you have practised saying the story through yourself first, so that you can work out the rhythm. Say the story through several times with the children, encouraging them to join in as much as possible.

Easter

Let's all clap hands!

Bold brave Peter?

Bold brave Peter: 'I'll stay around,
You know I will not let you down,
I'll stick by you right to the end,
I'll never leave you; you're my best friend.'

Poor sad Peter, lonely and scared:
'I don't know him; no, I don't care,
Never met him; who did you say?
I've never heard of him till today.'

- Maggie Barfield
- Matthew 26:69-75; Mark 14:66-72; Luke 22:56-62; John 18:15-18,25-27
- Humpty Dumpty
- Contrast Peter's actions and feelings by using your voice and body language - start loud, cheerful and standing boldly; then cower and use a trembling voice.

Easter morning

Poor Mary was sad. It had been so bad.
'My Jesus has died,' she sadly cried.
She went on her way on this Easter Day
To find Jesus' tomb but found an empty room!
Then two angels bright gave her quite a fright!
But the angels said, 'Jesus is not dead!'
She was filled with delight at the happy sight
And she went back to say, 'He's alive today!'
Hooray! Hooray! Hooray! Hooray!

- Angela Thompson
- Matthew 27:57 - 28:10; Mark 15:42 - 16:8; Luke 23:50 - 24:12; John 19:38 - 20:10
- Celebrate the resurrection of Jesus.

Easter

Mary was sad when Jesus died, Jesus died, Jesus died,
Mary was sad when Jesus died, Jesus died.
(Hold hands and walk round slowly in a circle.)

Mary went down to Jesus' tomb, Jesus' tomb, Jesus' tomb,
Mary went down to Jesus' tomb on Easter Day.
(Reverse direction, walk slowly back again.)

What a surprise he wasn't there, wasn't there, wasn't there,
What a surprise he wasn't there on Easter Day!
(Stand still, let go of hands, spread hands out in surprise, turn around.)

Jesus is alive today, alive today, alive today,
Jesus is alive today on Easter Day!
(Raise arms in praise on each line.)

Jesus is with us all day long, all day long, all day long
Jesus is with us all day long, every day!
(Hold hands again and skip around joyfully.)

- Angela Thompson
- Matthew 27:57 - 28:10; Mark 15:42 - 16:8; Luke 23:50 - 24:12; John 19:38 - 20:10
- The wheels on the bus
- A ring dance and story song

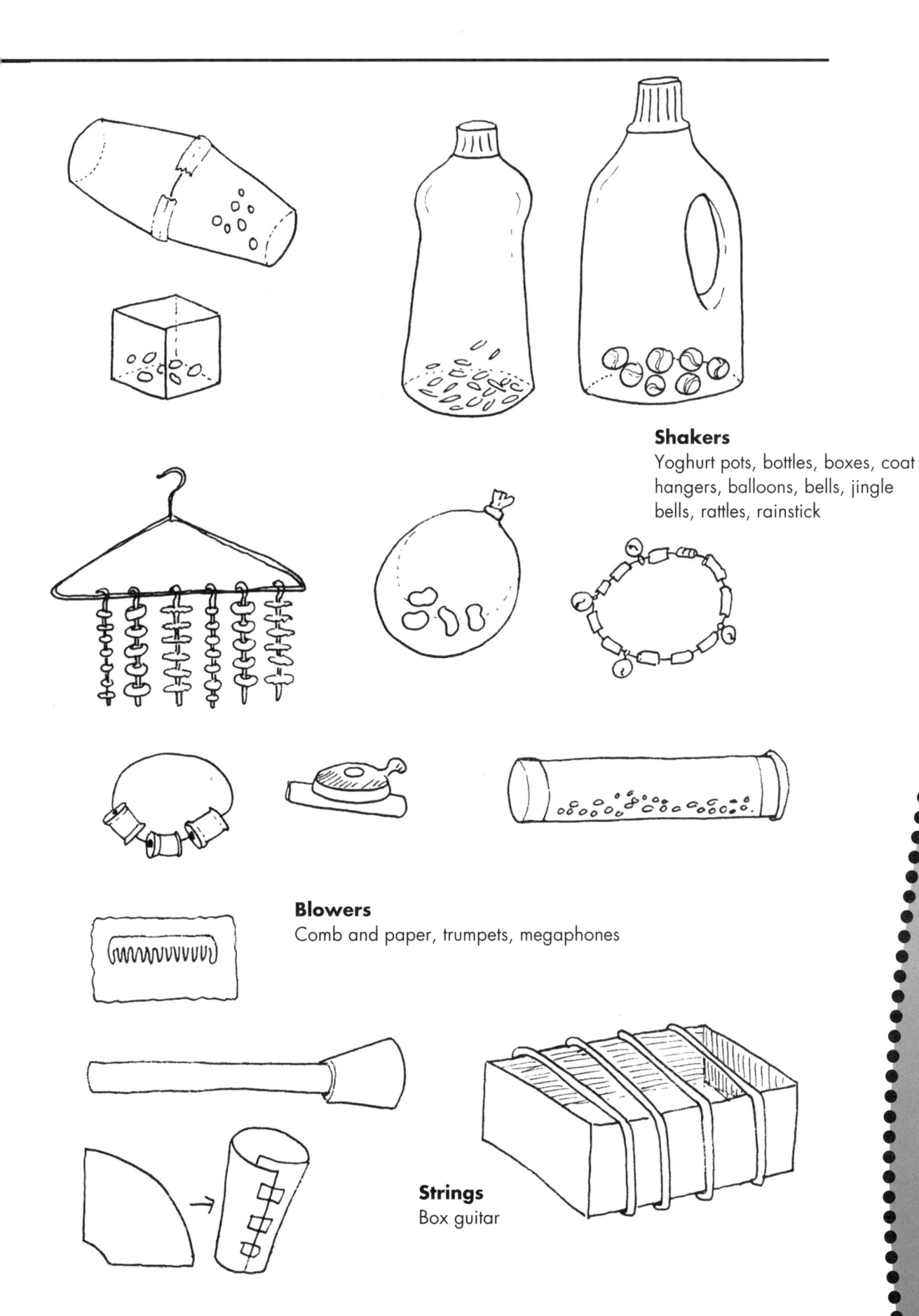

Shakers
Yoghurt pots, bottles, boxes, coat hangers, balloons, bells, jingle bells, rattles, rainstick

Blowers
Comb and paper, trumpets, megaphones

Strings
Box guitar

Make your own instruments

Let's all clap hands!

He's alive

We have seen him, he's alive,
We have seen him, he's alive,
We have seen him, he's alive,
Jesus is alive!

Verses:
Jesus walked the road with us,
Jesus walked the road with us,
Jesus walked the road with us,
We know he's alive!

He sat down to eat with us,
He sat down to eat with us,
He sat down to eat with us,
And we know he's alive!

He will always be with us,
He will always be with us,
He will always be with us,
Jesus is alive!

- Alison Gidney
- Mark 16:12,13; Luke 24:13-35
- Someone's brought a loaf of bread
- Encourage everyone to join in the chorus

Two friends

Two friends walking – down a dusty road.
Two friends talking, talking as they go.
Two friends feeling sad – Jesus has died.
Two friends puzzling – could he come alive?

Two friends looking round – a stranger joins them.
Two friends listening hard – he seems a special man.
Two friends telling him why they are upset.
Two friends asking him what the scriptures meant.

Two friends wondering – how can he be so wise?
Two friends feeling glad – with the stranger at their side.
Two friends, aching feet – nearly at Emmaus.
Two friends beg the stranger – 'Don't go. Stay here with us!'

Two friends light the lamps; the stranger breaks the bread.
Two friends recognise – it's Jesus! He's not dead!
Two friends hurrying – back along the road.
Two friends full of joy, laughing as they go.
Two friends tell their friends – 'Jesus is alive!'
Two friends tell their friends – 'We feel so good inside!'

- Jean Elliott
- Mark 16:12,13; Luke 24:13-35
- Walk along in pairs to re-enact this story rhyme; or 'walk' two pairs of fingers to copy the two friends.

Jesus listens

We can always talk to Jesus,
We can always talk to Jesus,
We can always talk to Jesus,
And we know he listens.

We can tell him how we're feeling,
We can tell him how we're feeling,
We can tell him how we're feeling,
And we know he listens.

We can ask him to help others,
We can ask him to help others,
We can ask him to help others,
And we know he listens.

- Jacquie Sibley
- Mark 16:12,13; Luke 24:13–35
- Bobby Shaftoe
- Apply the experience of the disciples to our own lives.

On Easter Day

Two friends were walking.
Two friends were talking.
Both of them feeling sad.
Jesus came walking.
Jesus came talking.
Then the two friends were glad!

- Jacquie Sibley
- Mark 16:12,13; Luke 24:13–35
- A before-and-after story rhyme

Jesus is alive!

Jesus is alive. *(Wave hands above head.)*
Jesus is alive. *(Wave hands.)*
We're so happy. *(Clap hands.)*
Jesus is alive. *(Wave hands.)*
(Sing it again with the actions and encourage the children to copy you.)

Jesus is with us. *(Stamp feet.)*
Jesus is with us. *(Stamp feet.)*
We're so happy. *(Clap hands.)*
Jesus is with us. *(Stamp feet.)*

Jesus loves and cares. *(Clap hands.)*
Jesus loves and cares. *(Clap hands.)*
We're so happy. *(Clap hands.)*
Jesus loves and cares. *(Clap hands.)*

- Jacquie Sibley
- Easter stories
- The farmer's in his den
- An action ring game.

Three times

'Do you love me, Peter?' Jesus said.
Peter looked at Jesus and nodded his head.
Yes, Lord, I love you, Jesus, I do!

'Do you love me, Peter?' Jesus said.
Peter looked at Jesus and nodded his head.
Yes, Lord, I love you, Jesus, I do!

'Do you love me, Peter?' Jesus said.
Peter looked at Jesus and nodded his head.
Yes, Lord, I love you, Jesus, I do!

'Do you love me, children? I love you,'
Jesus asks all of us, me and you.
Yes, Lord, I love you, Jesus, I do!

- Helen Burn
- John 21:5–19
- Repeat with a group response: 'Yes, Lord, we love you, Jesus, we do!'

Jesus is it you?

Jesus, Jesus, is it really you?
Look at my feet, look at my hands!
Jesus, Jesus, can it really be true?
Touch me. I am alive!
Jesus, Jesus, is it really you?
I'll eat some fish. See, I'm not a ghost!
Jesus, Jesus, can it really be true?
Look what it says in the Bible!
It is you. It really is true.

- Kirsty Lockhart

Easter

Easter

Let's all clap hands!

📖 Matthew 28:16-20; Mark 16:14-18; Luke 24:36-49; John 20:19-23; Acts 1:6-8

❗ Children can ask 'Jesus' the questions; his answers give the evidence they need to believe he is alive.

Weary fishermen

Seven weary fishermen saw someone burning sticks.
John said it was Jesus, then there were six.
Six weary fishermen said, 'Can he be alive?'
One could not believe it, then there were five.
Five weary fishermen, rowed for the shore.
Peter jumped into the sea, then there were four.
Four weary fishermen, bobbing on the sea.
One hauled up the net, then there were three.
Three weary fishermen had such a lot to do.
One pulled the boat ashore, then there were two.
Two weary fishermen, in the morning sun,
Staggered up the beach and there they found – just one!
One special person, with breakfast on a plate!
He shared out the bread and fish, enough for all eight!

✍ Rose Williams

📖 John 21:1-13

❗ A counting-down rhyme; act out the story using seven children to be fishermen plus one to be Jesus; or use play figures or puppets.

The promise

Jesus made a promise,
A promise to his friends:
'I will not leave you on your own,
You never need be all alone.
My friendship never ends.'

Jesus made a promise,
His Spirit soon to send.
'I will not leave you on your own,
You never need be all alone.
The Spirit is your friend.'

Jesus made a promise,
'He'll help in all you do.
I will not leave you on your own,
You never need be all alone.
His power will fill you too.'

Jesus made a promise,
'I'll keep it, never fear.
I will not leave you on your own,
You never need be all alone.
Just wait – he'll soon be here!'

✍ Marjory Francis

📖 Matthew 28:18-20; Mark 16:14-18; Luke 24:36-49; John 20:19-23; Acts 1:6-8

❗ Use this rhyme to consider the different aspects of the promise that Jesus gave to his followers; this could be used to review the situation before a Pentecost celebration.

The early church

Here is the church

Here is the church and here is the steeple,
(Criss cross fingers and fold inwards; lift two index fingers up.)
Open the door and here are the people.
(Open thumbs out; turn hands up and waggle fingers.)
Here is the parson going upstairs,
(Walk two fingers up the fingers on the other hand, like a ladder.)
And here he is a-saying his prayers.
(Hands together, eyes closed.)

Here are the people singing and praying,
(Waggle fingers; open mouth extra wide; hands together.)
Thinking and watching and listening and saying.
(Point to head, eyes, ears, mouth in turn.)
All shapes and sizes and ages together –
(Point round the room to everyone.)
A church made of people who care for each other!
(Spread out hands and arms in big circle.)

- First verse traditional; second verse Maggie Barfield
- Finger rhyme to show that the church is people not only a building

The Holy Spirit

God sent the Holy Spirit –
(Sway and wave arms.)
in the roaring wind.
(Make whooshing noise.)
God sent the Holy Spirit – *(Sway and wave arms.)*
in dancing orange flames.
(Make flame shape with hands.)
God sent the Holy Spirit –
(Sway and wave arms.)
in talking and in voices. *(Touch mouths.)*

We feel the wind, we see the flames and we can use our voices.

- Sheila Clift
- Acts 2:1–21
- An action rhyme to experience the symbols of the Holy Spirit

Receiving

We may not see you Jesus,
But we know that you are near,
And when we sing and talk to you,
We know you always hear.

You sent the Holy Spirit,
To make your promise clear,
That when we sing and talk to you,
We know you always hear.

- Sheila Clift
- Acts 2:1–21
- All things bright and beautiful
- Repeat the first verse at the end.

The early church

Let's all clap hands!

Peter said

Peter said,
'Jesus loves you.'
The people said,
'What can we do?'

Peter said,
'Talk to Jesus.'
The people said,
'Jesus, help us.'

Peter said,
'Jesus forgives you.'
The people said,
'Jesus, thank you.'

- Elizabeth Alty
- Acts 2:14–42
- Could be adapted for two voices or two groups to read.

Choose some helpers

Some Mummies and their children had very little food,
(Cup hands, shake head.)
Some Mummies and their children had very little food,
Some Mummies and their children had very little food,
So the people at the church gave them help. *(Hold hands out flat, palms up.)*

They chose seven men to serve out the food … *(Giving out action.)*
Yes, the people at the church gave them help. *(Hands out flat, palms up.)*

Now everybody's happy as they care for one another … *(Hugging action.)*
With the people at the church giving help. *(Hold hands out flat, palms up.)*

- Rachael Champness
- Acts 6:1–7
- An action story rhyme

Friends

You gave Paul a friend, *(Join hands in circle.)*
And you give us friends too. *(Lift hands up and down and look round at each other.)*
With friends we all feel happy. *(Let go hands and draw a smile in the air.)*
Let's say A BIG THANK YOU! *(Loudly and clearly, with hands raised.)*

- Susie Matheson
- Acts 9:1–19
- An action rhyme which can be used for a ring game. Adapt the first line by changing 'Paul' and this rhyme can be used with many other Bible stories.

Telling the good news

Long long ago when *Paul* was on earth,
Jesus sent him to cities all about.
He told him to tell them of Jesus' love,
Why he lived and died and rose for all of us.

Now it's today and *we* are here,
Jesus wants us to go both far and near,
Telling everyone we know of Jesus' love,
Why he lived and died and rose for all of us.

- Susie Matheson
- Life of Paul, from Acts
- Contrasting the life and mission of the apostles with ours.

Stephen

Stephen was a man who was kind and helpful,
Stephen was a man who showed he loved God.
Stephen was a man who looked after people,
Stephen was a man who served them their meals.
Stephen was a man who was kind and helpful,
Stephen was a man who showed he loved God.

Stephen was a man who gave out the money,
Stephen was a man who was always fair,
Stephen was a man who did the best he could,
Stephen was a man who was brave and strong.
Stephen was a man who was kind and helpful,
Stephen was a man who showed he loved God.

- Kathleen Crawford
- Acts 6, 7
- The repeated lines of this rhyme explain why Stephen behaved the way he did.

This is Good News

'This is Good News; this is Good News;'
Jesus came to say, Jesus came to say.
'This is Good News; this is Good News;
For you here today, for you here today.
The Holy Spirit has come to me,
For God the Father has chosen me
To bring Good News, to bring Good News
For everyone.'

This is Good News; this is Good News.
Jesus is my friend. Jesus is my friend.
This is Good News;. This is Good News.
God's love never ends. God's love never ends.
His Holy Spirit is helping me,
To tell my friends who Jesus is.
This is Good News; this is Good News,
For you and me.

- Jean Elliott
- Acts 2
- This is the day
- Peter's message on the day of Pentecost applies to every day of our lives!

At Pentecost

The Holy Spirit came at Pentecost,
In wind and fire and flame *(Wave arms.)* at Pentecost,
And everybody heard *(Cup ear.)* at Pentecost,
How Jesus kept his word.

The good news comes to say *(Cup ear.)* at Pentecost,
That Jesus lives today *(Raise arms.)* at Pentecost,
And everybody heard at Pentecost,
How Jesus kept his word.

- Sheila Clift
- Acts 2:1–21
- Kumbaya
- The second verse explains the meaning and significance of the first.

Let's all clap hands!

This way, that way

When Paul set off with Barnabas
They travelled far away.
They talked of Jesus everywhere,
They talked of him each day.
They travelled this way, that way,
Forwards and backwards,
Talking every day,
And many people came along
To hear what they would say.

They had such happy news to tell
They wanted all to know
That Jesus is the greatest friend
That anyone could know
They talked in this town, that town
Round about town,
Talking every day,
And many people came along
To hear what they would say.

When Paul went home with Barnabas
They still had news to say
They'd been to visit all their friends
To help them live God's way
They'd travelled this way, that way,
Forwards and backwards,
Talking every day:
'Jesus loves you. Come and be
A friend for him today!'

Maggie Barfield

Acts 13—14

Over the briny sea/ The day I went to sea

The early missionary journeys can sound repetitive so this song turns that repetitive pattern into a positive feature.

Yes, yes, yes!

Paul and Timothy were walking all around,
Talking about Jesus to everyone they found,
Talking about Jesus – *Yes, yes, yes!*
Talking about Jesus – Yes, yes, yes!

Many people came to hear and welcomed them with glee,
Many joined the church – it was wonderful to see,
Wonderful to see – *Yes, yes, yes!*
Talking about Jesus – Yes, yes, yes!

They wanted to go this way – but getting there was slow,
They wanted to go that way – but God told them 'No!
Got to go God's way – *Yes, yes, yes!*
Talking about Jesus – Yes, yes, yes!

Paul had a dream and God showed the way to go,
Across the sea to Philippi so everyone could know,
Jesus is the best friend – *Yes, yes, yes!*
Talking about Jesus – Yes, yes, yes!

Then, Paul and Timothy were walking all around,
Talking about Jesus to everyone they found,
Talking about Jesus – *Yes, yes, yes!*
Talking about Jesus – Yes, yes, yes!

Malc' Halliday

Acts 16:1–15

Everyone can join in the repeated lines of this story rhyme.

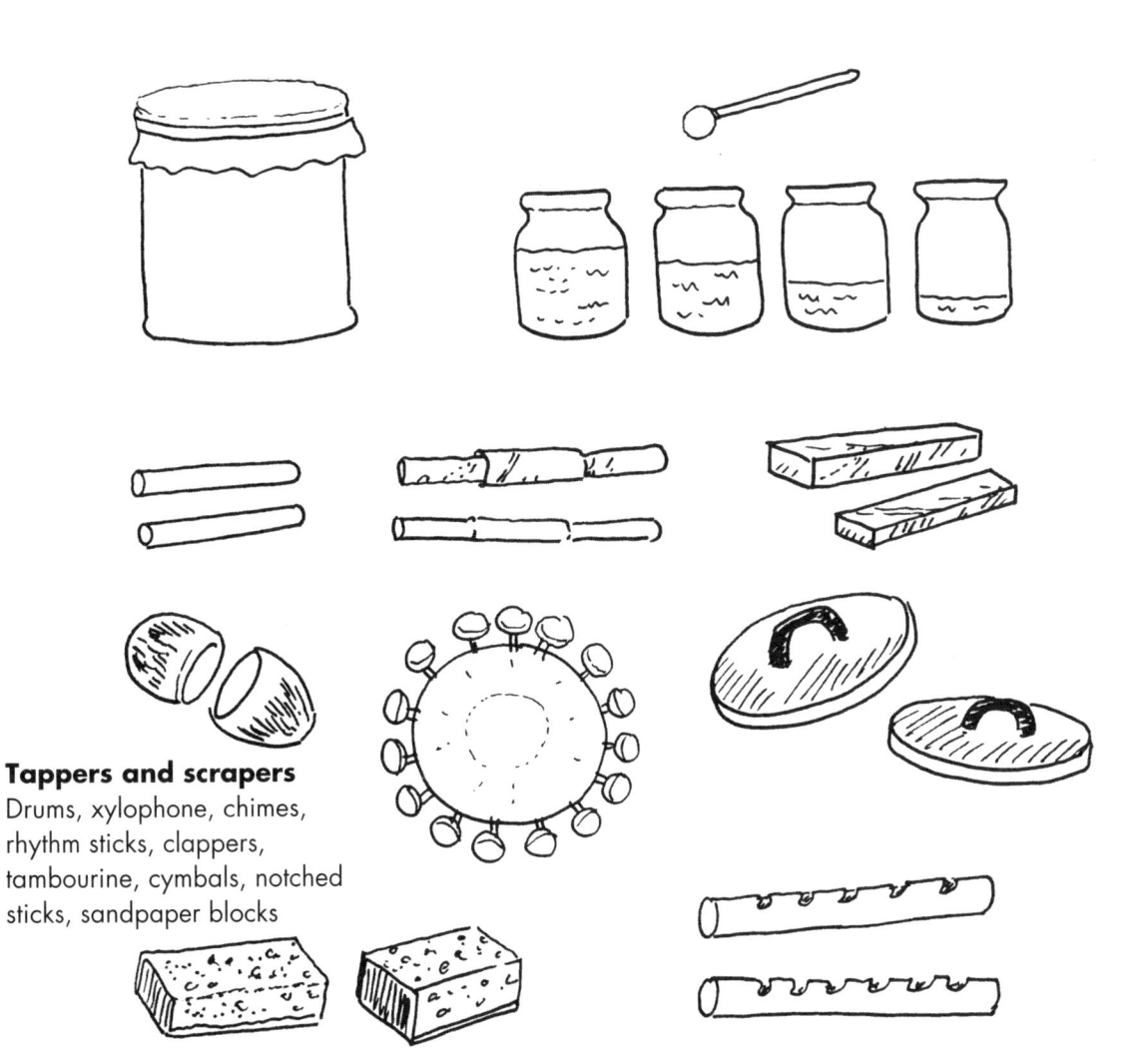

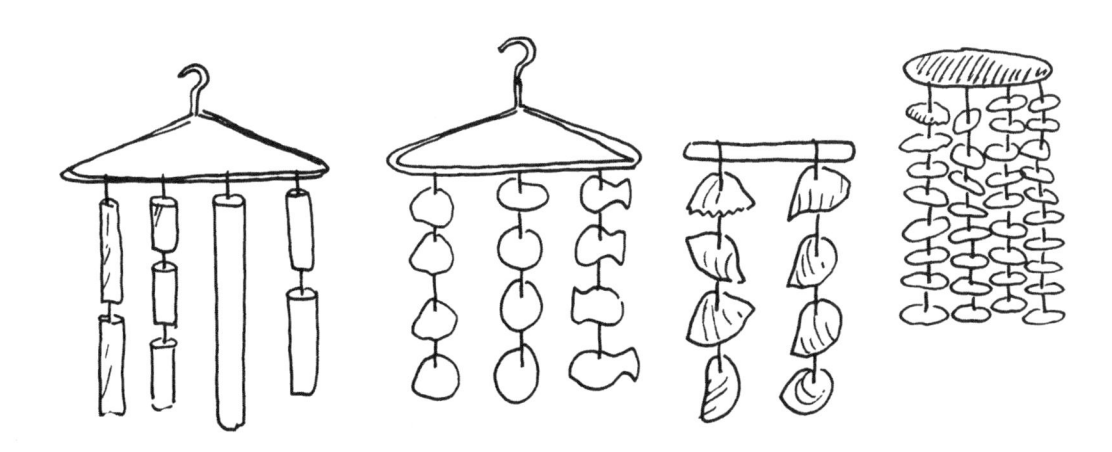

Tappers and scrapers
Drums, xylophone, chimes, rhythm sticks, clappers, tambourine, cymbals, notched sticks, sandpaper blocks

Wind
Foil chimes, dough chimes, shell chimes

Make your own instruments

Let's all clap hands!

Come to the church

Come to the church, come with your friends,
See how God's family grows.
Paul tells us about Jesus,
See how God's family grows,
See how God's family grows.

Jason is here and so are his friends.
Rich and poor agree –
Joining God's church is the best thing to do,
To be part of God's family,
To be part of God's family. Yeah!

- Elizabeth Alty
- Acts 17:1-9
- Mary, Mary quite contrary
- Improvise a simple dance to go with this story song.

Let's join in!

We want to be part of the Jesus family so –
Let's join in!
We want to be part of the Jesus family so –
Let's join in! Let's join in! Let's join in!
We want to be part of the Jesus family so –
Lets join in!

Thank you Jesus for all your church, we –
All join in!
Thank you Jesus for all your church, we –
All join in! All join in! All join in!
Thank you Jesus for all your church, we –
All join in!

- Elizabeth Alty
- Acts 17:1-9
- A praise shout.

Shh!

Shh! Shh! Paul is speaking.
Shh! Shh! He talks all day!
Shh! Shh! He tells of Jesus.
Shh! Shh! Let's all pray!

- Elizabeth Alty
- Acts 17:1-9
- Pretend to be part of the crowd listening to Paul – you all want to hear every word!

Read the Bible!

Paul and Silas told the people,
'Jesus is God's special person.'
They all listened to what Paul said,
Checked by reading in their Bibles!
'Jesus is God's special person!'
They said, 'We will be his friends too.'

- Christine Orme
- Acts 17:10-15
- A short story rhyme, showing that the Bible confirmed the message of good news.

Paul and Silas

Paul and Silas sail across the sea.
I like you *(Bow.)* and you like me. *(Bow.)*
They meet Timothy and walk a long way.
'Now we're three good friends,' they say. *(Bow. Put left hand down.)*

Paul's alone now, feeling sad.
'I wish I had my friends here to make me glad.'
Silas and Timothy sail across the sea.
'Now we're all together, we're happy as can be!'

- Margaret Spivey
- Acts 18:4,5

The early church

> An action rhyme to play in groups of three; at the end, all hold hands and dance round together.

Paul's new friends

Here is Paul talking to his friends.
(Hold one hand upright, waggle fingers.)
They like to talk of Jesus.
(Move hand in open and shut fashion, to symbolise chatting, then point upwards to Jesus.)
When Paul has to go they sadly say goodbye.
(Make waving motion, and move to next place.)

Here is Paul, meeting someone new.
(Hold up one finger and wiggle it towards finger on other hand.)
They like to learn of Jesus,
(Cup ear.)
Now they are friends of Jesus.
(Cross hands over chest.)

> Joy Chalke
> Acts 18:7-11,18-23
> A finger rhyme; or move round the room as you tell the story.

Paul's travels

Paul loved to tell all his good friends
That Jesus' love would never end.
So off he went, first to Justus,
And then the family of Crispus.

Paul went on a sailing ship
And went to Ephesus on a trip.
His new friends said, 'Please speak to us
And tell us all about Jesus.'

To every friend he told this news,
'My friend Jesus cares for you!' *(Point round the room to each other.)*

> Angela Thompson
> Acts 18: 7-11,18-23
> An overview of Paul's missionary journey and some of the people he met.

Paul's story

I was walking **(I was walking…)**
(Trudge in place.)
Cross and hot **(Cross and hot…)**
(Wipe forehead.)
Hunting Christians *(Peer around.)*
Hated them a lot. *(Thumbs down.)*
Bright light over me *(Shield eyes.)*
Down I fell. *(Fall down.)*
Heard a voice calling,
(Cup hand to ear.)
My heart stood still. *(Hand to heart.)*
It was Jesus calling! *(Cup hand to ear.)*
Jesus was alive! *(Wave hands in air.)*
My life had been all wrong
(Thumbs down.)
Now it could be right! *(Thumbs up.)*
Up I jumped. *(Jump up.)*
I had work to do!
(Rub hands together.)
Telling people everywhere,
(Point to each other.)
Telling all of you Jesus is alive!
(Wave hands in air.)
He makes me brave and strong.
(Show muscles.)
Jesus is my friend *(Hand to heart.)*
I'll say it all day long.
(Hands outstretched.)

> Mary Houlgate
> Acts 26
> An action story rhyme; the leader says each phrase with everyone repeating the words and doing the actions.

The early church

Let's all clap hands!

God's Spirit

If you're scared or angry,
(Make appropriate faces.)
If all your friends have gone,
(Shrug sadly.)
Call upon God's Spirit, *(Raise hands.)*
He will make you strong.
(Show muscles.)

God loves each and every one, *(Point at each other.)*
He wants to change our lives, *(Spin your hands over each other.)*
He gives us joy and peace within,
(Clasp heart.)
And makes us good *(Thumbs up.)* and wise. *(Tap head.)*

Thank you God! *(Clap for each word.)*

Thank you Spirit, you bring us love.
When we are sad, you bring us love.
When we are lonely, you bring us love.
(Encourage the children to add other times when we can know God's Spirit will help us. End with:)
Thank you Spirit, you change our lives,
Because you bring us love.

- Mary Houlgate
- Stories from Acts
- An action rhyme.

Timothy

Timothy, **Tim**othy, **Tim**othy, **Tim**,
He was a **help**er and **I'll** be like **him**.
Helping at **home** wher**ev**er I **can**,
I want to **be** like that **Tim**othy **man**!

- Christine Orme
- Story of Timothy
- A simple rhyme to help children learn about one of Paul's friends; stress the syllables in bold print.

Onesimus and Philemon

Jesus helped Onesimus;
He will help us too!
Jesus helped Onesimus;
Choose right things to do.
And if he helped Onesimus
Say sorry and go home,
Jesus will help us
We're never on our own.

Jesus helped Philemon;
He will help us too!
Jesus helped Philemon;
Choose right things to do.
And if he helped Philemon
Welcome back his slave,
Jesus will help us
Do right and be brave.

- Christine Orme
- Colossians 4:9; Philemon
- Ten Green Bottles
- A story song.

The early church

80

A child's life

God is there!

When I fall and hurt my elbow,
When I have a horrid dream,
When my brother's being nasty,
When a spider makes me scream,
When I stamp and lose my temper,
When I think nobody cares–
   Who is there?
   GOD IS THERE!

When I see a baby puppy,
When my best friend comes to play,
When I wear my favourite T-shirt,
When I have a brilliant day,
When I hear a funny story,
When the sun shines bright and fair–
   Who is there?
   GOD IS THERE!

When the day seems long and dreary,
And I'm feeling glum and sad,
When I need someone to cuddle,
And when everything seems bad,
When I want someone to love me,
And I feel that no one cares–
   Who is there?
   GOD IS THERE!

When I'm feeling full of troubles,
And I don't know what to say,
When I'm feeling so unhappy,
And those thoughts won't go away,
When my tears just keep on coming,
And it all seems so unfair–
   Who is there?
   GOD IS THERE!

Maggie Barfield

Select verses to stress positive or negative feelings; this rhyme complements 'Who was there?' about the life of Joseph on page 25.

Why, oh why?

Everyone likes Gemma,
Ray has friends galore,
Lucy says she's going to marry,
Christopher or Paul,
It seems that everyone makes friends
As easy as can be,
Oh, why are all these easy things
So difficult for me?

At breaktime, I feel lonely,
I'd like to go and play,
But everyone is busy,
So I keep right out the way.
It seems that everyone knows how
To join in – except me.
Oh, why is what I'd like to do
So difficult for me?

I wish I was not timid,
I wish I was not shy,
I wish I could shout out in class
And wave my hand up high.
It seems that everyone is brave –
That's how I'd like to be.
Oh, why, oh, why is everything
So difficult for me?

Dear Jesus, please be with me,
I like to know you care.
When everything is hard for me,
It's so good to know you're there.
I'm glad you're close beside me, Lord,
A friend, to hold my hand.
I'm glad you know just how I feel –
You always understand.

Maggie Barfield

Things don't always go right but we can always rely on Jesus.

A child's life

Let's all clap hands!

No food

Her legs are like sticks,
Her ribs show through,
Her tummy looks fat,
But she's got no food.

Help all children, dear Father,
Who are hungry today,
And help me to help them
In some little way.

Maggie Barfield

A child's response to a famine photograph.

Two busy fathers

Two busy fathers walking down the street,
One named David, one named Pete.
To the office, David. To the factory, Pete.
Come home David. Come home Pete.

Fathers with their children going to the park,
One named Stephen, one named Mark.
To the playground, Stephen. To the duck pond, Mark.
Home time, Stephen. Home time, Mark.

Two sleepy fathers early in the day,
One named Wesley, one named Ray.
Read the paper, Wesley. Feed the baby, Ray.
WAKE UP, WESLEY! WAKE UP, RAY!

Maggie Barfield

Different family styles; all dads are different.

This and that

Sometimes I *smack* when I'm angry
And things aren't going my way,
But when I'm happy, I *clap* for joy
And shout hooray!

Sometimes I *kick* when I'm angry
And things aren't going my way,
But when I'm happy I *skip* for joy
And shout hooray!

Sometimes I *stamp* when I'm angry
And things aren't going my way,
But when I'm happy, I *march* for joy
And shout hooray!

Mary Houlgate

Our feelings sometimes overwhelm us but we can change negative emotions for positive.

I am growing

Once, I was a baby. I cried and rolled about,
But now, look at what I do, I run and jump and SHOUT!
I am growing!
Once I was so tiny and all I did was crawl.
But now look at what I do, I stretch and stand up tall.
I am growing!

Elizabeth Alty

Child's growth and development.

Two of us

Two little eyes to look at friends,
Two little ears to hear them talk,
Two little lips to smile with them,
Two little feet to go for a walk,
Two little hands to hold their hands
And one little heart to give my love.

Susie Matheson
Two little eyes to look to God
Being with others.

Superstar!

Every day, come what may,
No matter who you are,
Jesus thinks that you are great –
You are a superstar!
Jesus thinks you're wonderful!
He loves you through and through!
Night and day in every way,
He loves you, just as YOU!

Maggie Barfield
Each of us is special and known to Jesus.

Who cares?

Sometimes children get upset and cry, *(Shake your head and run fingers down cheeks to suggest tears.)*
They can be sure that someone's nearby; *(Hug yourself.)*
Someone who cares, *(Hold hands out.)*
Someone I know. *(Tap nose.)*
That someone is my friend Jesus. *(Point upwards.)*

Christine Wright
Mark 5:21–43
Jesus is with us in bad times.

I don't know

I don't know where I left my socks,
I've lost my other shoe,
I don't know what I had to take,
Or what I had to do.
I'm thinking of so many things
But this one thing is true –
I know you never forget me
And I remember you.

I've put my pencils somewhere,
And I really ought to know.
It's like this every morning
When it comes to 'Time to go!'
I'm thinking of so many things
But this, I know is true –
I know you never forget me
And I remember you.

Maggie Barfield
We might get muddled and forgetful but God is always reliable.

My family

Thank you for my family,
Thank you God that they love me,
Thank you that they care for me,
Cook my chips and make my tea. *(Let go of hands, rub tummies, lick lips happily. Hold hands and dance again.)*
Thank you for my family,
Thank you God that they love me.

Angela Thompson
Twinkle, twinkle little star
Dance and sing your thanks.

A child's life

Let's all clap hands!

Watching the wind

I look through my window and what do I see?
The grass and the flowers are waving to me,
The wind gently swaying the leaves of the trees
And butterflies dancing along with the breeze.

Bustling and gusting and twisting around
The wind's playing wild games all over the town.
It's catching the dry dust and tossing it round
And chasing the litter along on the ground.

The wind's sneaking in through the joins of my clothes.
It's making my ears ache and hurting my nose,
With sharp icy fingers, it's freezing my toes
And my knees and my chin and my cheeks, as it blows.

Nothing is stirring; the wind's gone away,
No huffing or puffing or bluster today,
No soft breath of fresh air to whisper and play,
Just quiet and stillness and calmness all day.

Maggie Barfield

Experience of nature.

The library

I'm going to the library
To choose a story book.
There are hundreds and thousands there
Around me as I look.
There are funny tales and mysteries
Of children big and small.
There's up-to-date and long ago –
I want to read them all.

The Bible's like a library
Of story books to read:
A shepherd looking for his sheep;
A farmer sowing seed;
A man gets mugged and left to die;
A precious pearl is sold;
And weeds get muddled up with wheat
In stories Jesus told.

Maggie Barfield

Comparing a library full of books with a book which is a library.

Art

Thank you, God, for painting, drawing,
Things to make and things to do.
Thank you, God, for colours, patterns,
Pictures I can make for you.
I'm happy being me!

Maggie Barfield

We are all creative beings because God made us that way.

If you wanna be wise

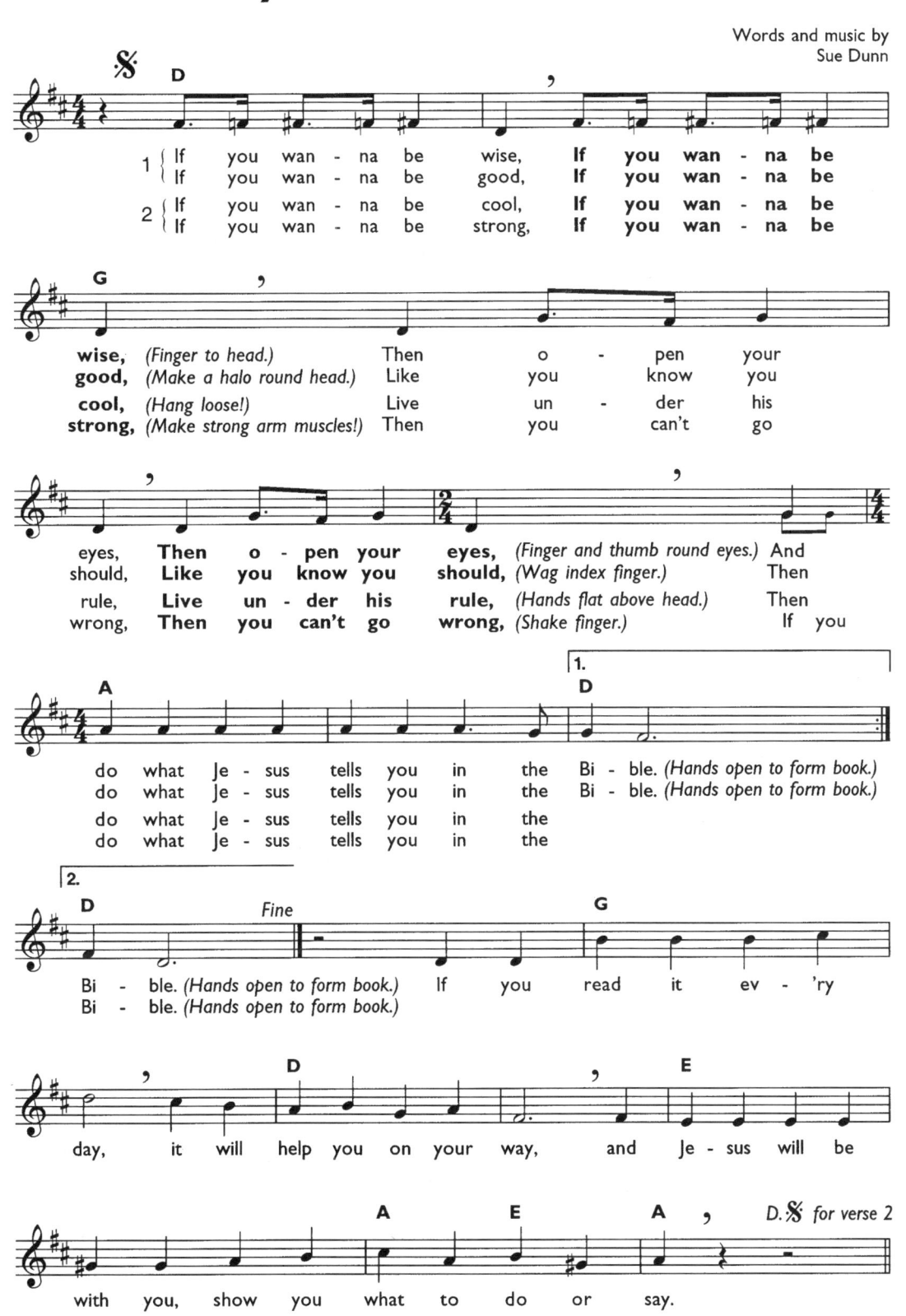

Words and music by Sue Dunn

1. If you wanna be wise, If you wanna be wise, (Finger to head.) Then open your eyes, Then open your eyes, (Finger and thumb round eyes.) And if you do what Jesus tells you in the Bible. (Hands open to form book.)

   If you wanna be good, If you wanna be good, (Make a halo round head.) Like you know you should, Like you know you should, (Wag index finger.) Then if you do what Jesus tells you in the Bible. (Hands open to form book.)

2. If you wanna be cool, If you wanna be cool, (Hang loose!) Live under his rule, Live under his rule, (Hands flat above head.) Then if you do what Jesus tells you in the Bible. (Hands open to form book.)

   If you wanna be strong, If you wanna be strong, (Make strong arm muscles!) Then you can't go wrong, Then you can't go wrong, (Shake finger.) If you do what Jesus tells you in the Bible. (Hands open to form book.)

If you read it ev'ry day, it will help you on your way, and Jesus will be with you, show you what to do or say.

© Scripture Union

Let's all clap hands!

A child's life

Let's all clap hands!

Camping out

In our tent we're camping out,
We're living out of doors:
Poles and ropes to hold it up
And canvas roof and walls.

We put our tent up in a field
But we did not take care.
We left the field gate open so
The sheep got everywhere.

The rain poured down all through one night,
Drum-drumming on all sides;
But curled up snugly in our tent
We all were dry inside.

Next day the clouds had blown away,
The day was bright and breezy.
We picnicked in our sunny field –
Our camping out was easy!

Too soon our holiday was done.
We packed our tent away,
Said goodbye to our outdoor life –
But we'll camp again one day.

Maggie Barfield

A humorous holiday experience; link to Bible stories of nomadic life or Festival of Shelters; contrast the short-term holiday with the regular lifestyle of many Bible characters.

I like books

I like books! I like books!
Lift-the-flap books, story books, rhyme books,
Touch-and-feel books, what's-the-time? books,
Books with pictures, books with sound,
Books about things I see all around,
I like books! I like books!

What-a-surprise! books, use-your-eyes books,
Shut-the-door books, find-out-more books,
Books with pictures, books with sound,
Books about things I see all around,
I like books! I like books!

Concertina books, funny books, sad books,
You-can-make-it books, bath books, rag books,
Books with pictures, books with sound,
Books about things I see all around,
I like books! I like books!

Christine Orme

Acts 17:10–15

Discovery rhyme about the different types of book; use as an introduction to God's book, the Bible.

Feeling happy

It's easy to feel happy on a bright and happy day
When I'm feeling bright and cheerful and the grumps are far away
It's harder to be cheerful when the whole day turns out bad
And the grumps are all around me and I'm crotchety and sad.
But no matter what I feel like and no matter what the day
There is one who's always with me and who never goes away
There's one who thinks I'm brilliant and who loves me all the time
Now, can you guess who he can be, this special friend of mine?

Maggie Barfield

Everyday life; can the children guess the answer without too much prompting?

Playing

This is the way I throw my ball, up and catch, up and catch,
This is the way I throw my ball, up and catch.
Do you think Jesus played with a ball?
Up and catch, up and catch.
Do you think Jesus played with a ball?
Up and catch.

This is the way I run around, run and run, run and run,
This is the way I run around, run and run.
Do you think Jesus ran around? Ran and ran, ran and ran.
Do you think Jesus ran around? Ran and ran.

This is the way I clap and sing, la, la, la, la, la, la, *(And clap.)*
This is the way I clap and sing, la, la, la.
Do you think Jesus clapped and sang?
La, la, la, la, la, la,
Do you think Jesus clapped and sang?
La, la, la.

Rachael Champness

Here we go round the mulberry bush

Playing and life in NT times were similar to the way we play today.

When I'm sad

Flowers and pets and people die;
It makes me sad; it makes me cry.
Jesus, I'm glad to know you're near
To comfort me and soothe my tears.

Maggie Barfield

Bereavement; everything that is living, dies; we need to know it's OK to feel sad and to know Jesus is there with us when we feel that way; he doesn't reject us.

Day by day

On Monday it was snowing.
I threw snowballs with my friend.

On Tuesday it was stormy.
Would the thunder never end?

On Wednesday it was windy
And my hat blew down the street.

On Thursday it was raining –
Lots of puddles, what a treat!

On Friday it was foggy
And I couldn't see a thing.

On Saturday the sun came out
And birds began to sing.

What a lot of weather:
Some warm, some cold, some grey.

And now today is Sunday –
What's the weather like today?

Malc' Halliday

A humorous rhyme to explore the variety of weather in God's world; if you meet on a day other than Sunday, shift all the days around so you end by saying 'today is ---day' as your meeting day.

All I need

Thank you, God, for my home,
You give me what I need.
Thank you, God, for the clothes I wear,
You give me what I need.
Thank you, God, for my food each day,
You give me what I need.

Peggy Gibson

A prayer with a response for all to join in; extend the prayer by adding suggestions from your group for other things they would like to mention.

A child's life

A child's life

Let's all clap hands!

Hello God. It's me.

It's fun getting up in the morning
And starting a brand new day.
It's fun looking out of the window.
When I'm putting my clothes on
I say, 'Hi, God! It's me!'

It's fun in the park when I'm walking.
I scuffle the leaves with my feet.
It's fun to do painting at playgroup,
Then come home for good things to eat
And say, 'That was nice, God!'

It's cosy and warm in my bedroom
When I go for my afternoon rest.
I look at some books before sleeping
And I talk to God too. He's the best!
'I love you, God!'

It's fun with my brother and sister
When they come home from school later on.
It's fun having tea all together
And soon the good food is all gone.
'Thank you, God!'

It's fun to hear stories at bedtime
And know that I'm never alone,
'Look after me tonight, God! Amen.'

Christine Orme

Through the day experiences

Move it!

Clap your hands, touch your toes,
Clean your teeth, blow your nose.
Click your fingers, stretch up high,
Say 'Hello' or wave goodbye.
Switch on the light, open a door,
Dig the garden, sweep the floor.
Bake a cake, then eat your tea,
Bounce a ball or skip with me.
Drive a car, row a boat,
Scratch an itch, fasten your coat.
Hug a teddy, stroke the cat,
Brush your hair, put on a hat.
Paint a picture, write your name,
Build a tower, play a game,
Open a parcel or a jar,
Bang a drum, play a guitar.

© Kathleen Crawford, from *Zac and the Multi-coloured spidajig*, SU.)

Mark 3:1–6

Experiment with some of the amazing things we can do with our bodies.

Friends

Good to see you

We are so pleased to see you,
Everyone is thrilled!
Look, sit here beside me,
Chairs will soon be filled.
Here's the book we follow.
We start the service there.
Sing the song, it's easy!
Now we say a prayer.
Orange juice? A biscuit?
We're very glad you've come.
Enjoy your visit with us.
Welcome! Welcome! Welcome!

Rose Williams

A rhyme to welcome new or regular members to the group.

Friends

If you give your smile to me,
I'll give my smile to you.
Then everyone can see
Just what a smile can do.

If you wave to me,
I will wave to you.
Then everyone can see
Just what a wave can do.

If you shake hands with me,
I'll shake hands with you.
Then everyone can see
Just what a handshake can do.

Sheila Clift

Acts 2:1–21

Improvise actions as suggested in the rhyme.

Friends together

If you're looking for a friend then find one now,
If you're looking for a friend then find one now,
Take your new friend by the hand, find a space where you can stand,
If you're looking for a friend, then find one now.

If you're happy with your friend, dance round and round,
If you're happy with your friend, dance round and round,
Give a smile to everyone, laugh together, have some fun,
If you're happy with your friend, dance round and round.

If Jesus is your friend then shout 'Hooray!'
He'll be with you when you play, he'll be with you all the day,
If Jesus is your friend then shout 'Hooray!'
If Jesus is your friend then shout 'Hooray!'

If you want a friend called Jesus, tell him now,
If you want a friend called Jesus, tell him now,
He is listening every day, he will hear you when you say,
That you want to be his friend – just tell him now.

Dorothy Johnson

Matthew 9:9-13

She'll be coming round the mountain

Follow the action instructions in the rhyme.

Let's all clap hands!

When we love you

Thank you that we can be friends with others
When we love you, Lord Jesus.
Thank you for the people who help us share
When we love you, Lord Jesus.
Thank you that there is so much to give and to receive
When we love you, Lord Jesus.

- Margaret Cluley
- Deuteronomy 14:22-29; 16:18-20
- a prayer with a response for all to join in; add further lines as suggested within your group.

Sharing friends

Jesus wants us all to share, all to share, all to share,
Jesus wants us all to share, every day.

He will help us when it's hard, when it's hard, when it's hard,
He will help us when it's hard, every day.

- Margaret Cluley
- Deuteronomy 14:22-29; 16:18-20
- London Bridge
- A little song which is easy to remember; encourage children to learn it by heart so they will have it 'with them' when they need to be reassured.

What are friends like?

Friends are kind,
Friends are fun,
Friends can talk and listen, too.
Friends can help,
Friends can hug,
You like them and they like you.

Friends can share,
Friends can care,
Friends can play with you all day.
Friends say sorry,
Friends forgive,
Friends don't sulk or run away.

Friends are good, friends are great,
Friends can laugh and joke with you.
Friends are true,
Friends are fond,
Friends enjoy the things you do.

I like friends, don't you?

- Formerly in *Sing, say and move*
- Do a thumbs-up sign every time you say or hear the word 'friends'.

What can friends do together?

Friends can walk together,
(Walk fingers along.)
Laugh and talk together,
(Smile and 'talk' with hands.)
Thanks for friends!

Friends can cry together,
(Look sad and mime crying.)
Have great fun together,
(Dance fingers about.)
Thanks for friends!

Friends can stay together,
(Link forefingers.)
Sing and pray together,
(Hands together.)
Thanks for friends!

- Formerly in *Sing, say and move*
- Children can mime actions and say the last line in each verse.

Helping friends

If I help you *(Offer right hand to person next to you.)*
And you help me, *(Offer left hand to person next to you and join hands.)*
Oh how happy we will be,
Helping others every day *(Still holding hands, shake them up and down.)*
In our work and in our play.

- Margaret Cluley
- A rhyme which helps us practise being friendly and welcoming.

Best friends

We love friends to play with,
At any time of day.
Some we have at nursery,
Some live down our way.
But Jesus is our best friend,
Our saviour and our king.
Oh isn't that so wonderful!
It makes us want to sing!

- Angela Thompson
- Acts 18:7-11,18-23
- Sing a song of sixpence
- A song to sing or pray together.

We hope you'll stay

There's a girl called *Sophie*, she is here today,
We're glad *Sophie* is our friend and we hope she'll stay.
There's a boy called *Robert*, he is here today,
We're glad *Robert* is our friend, and we hope he'll stay.

- Margaret Spivey
- a getting-to-know-you game

Hello, hello

Hello, hello, let me greet you. *(Wave.)*
How are you? It's nice to meet you! *(Shake hands.)*
Come on in and sit down with us! *(Gesture towards a seat.)*
Very nice to meet you! *(Shake hands or nod heads.)*

- Mary Houlgate
- Acts
- Bobby Shaftoe
- A welcoming and getting-to-know-you game and song.

Who will be a friend?

Martin's all alone,
Martin's all alone,
Who will be his friend,
So he's not alone?

Together we can dance!
Together we can sing!
We praise God together,
He gives us everything.

- Mary Houlgate
- Acts
- The farmer's in his den
- Encourage a volunteer to lead him back into the circle. Then dance around to this verse.

Food and drink

Let's all clap hands!

Welcome everybody!

Welcome, welcome, everyone here.
Welcome James and welcome Hayley
Welcome Lee and welcome Martin.
We are glad you're here today.

- Christine Wright
- Luke 18:15-17
- Humpty Dumpty, taking liberties with the rhythm to fit in the children's names.
- A getting-to-know-you and welcoming game; use the names of children in your group and repeat as many times as necessary to include everyone in this welcome.

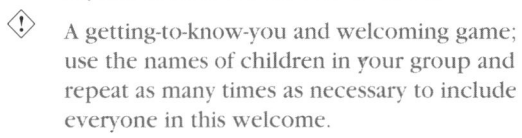

Helping

I can help others, I can help others,
Yes, yes, yes I can.
I can care for them, I can care for them,
Yes, yes, yes I can.
Point to your fingers! Point to your head!
Point to your mouth and point to your hands.
Clap your hands together: 1 - 2 - 3!
I want God to use me!

- Rachael Champness
- Acts 6:1-7
- Wind the bobbin up
- An action song to help children think about what it means to be friends.

Food and drink

Bread for life

Toast for my breakfast,
Sandwiches for tea,
Thin bread and butter
When Granny stays with me.

Brown bread or white bread?
Long loaves or short?
Look in the shopping bag
To see what Mummy's bought!

Thank you, farmers,
For growing golden wheat,
So that all the bakers
Can make us bread to eat.

Thank you, God,
For keeping us fed
With so many, lovely
Different kinds of bread.

- Christine Orme
- Luke 11:1-8
- Use bread as a staple food; variety of breads; cycle of growth and production

Lovely bread

Bread, bread, lovely bread.
Bread to cut and bread to spread
With honey, butter, fruit or cheese,
Lovely bread! More please!

Fish, fish, tasty fish,
Sitting waiting on my dish.
Herring, whiting, plaice and cod,
For tasty fish, we thank you God.

- Pam Macnaughton

Let the children come

Words by Maggie Barfield
Music traditional

We're going to see Jesus, see Jesus, see Jesus, we're going to see Jesus, wherever he may be. Why don't you come and join us, and join us, and join us, we're going to see Jesus. Why don't you come and see?

Words © Scripture Union

I'm building a house

Words by Maggie Barfield
Music by Scripture Union

I'm building a house, with four strong walls, two shiny windows, and a smart front door, I'm putting on a roof, to keep it dry, it's going to be a good house, by and by. It's a lovely little house, now, don't you see? It's a lovely little house, don't you agree?

© Scripture Union

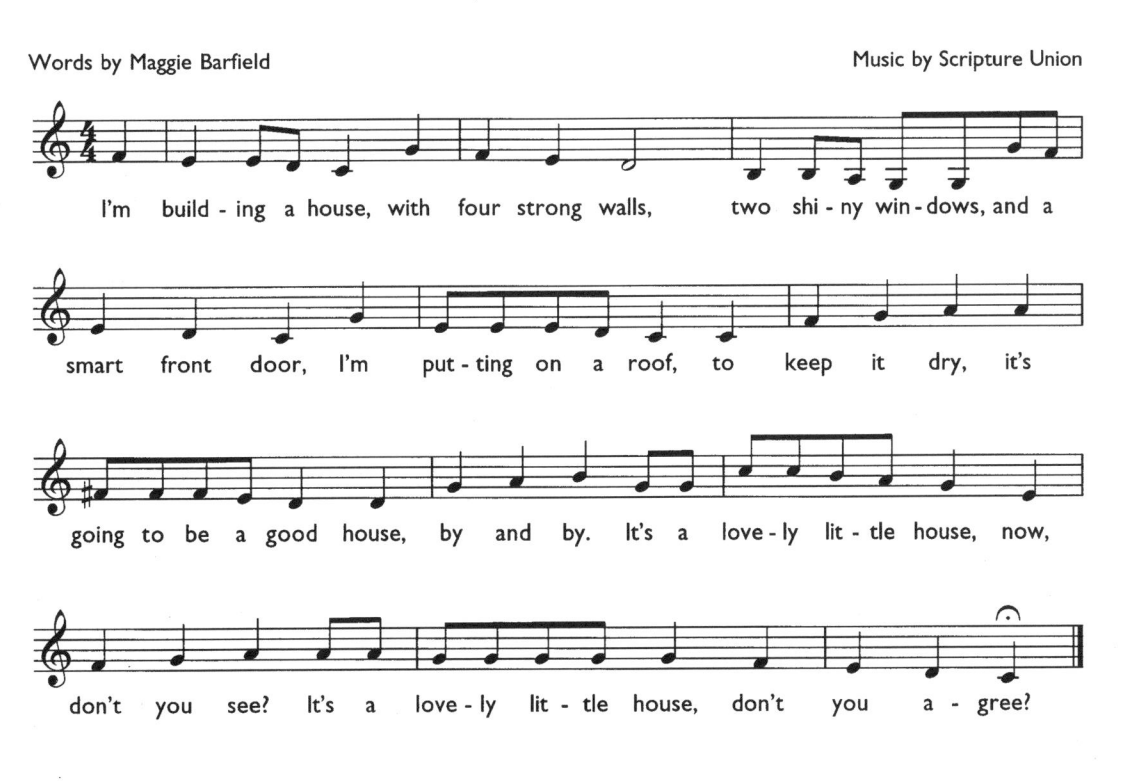

Let's all clap hands!

Food and drink

Let's all clap hands!

📖 John 6:1-15

❗ Stories about food in Bible times; this rhyme relates biblical meals with the type of foods children today may know.

Here and there

What's to eat today, Mum?
Sausage pie
Or beans on toast,
Egg and chips
Or Sunday roast.
Strawberry ice
Or treacle pud,
Apple crumble
Tasting good.

**But in a country far away
No need to ask your mother twice.
What's to eat today, Mum?
Plain boiled rice.**

What's to drink today, Mum?
Coca cola,
Cherryade,
Cup of tea
Just freshly made,
Cool white milk
Or chocolate hot,
Coffee from
A silver pot.

**But in a country far away
The answer to a son or daughter,
What's to drink today, Mum?
Dirty water.**

What to do today, Mum?
With your friends
Go off to play,
Cricket, football,
That's the way.
Colouring,
Computer fun,
Films and TV
Till day's done.

*But in a country far away,
No need to make a fuss.
What to do today, Mum?
Work for us.*

Where to sleep today, Mum?
In a cot
Or in a bed,
Cosy pillow
At my head,
In a bunk
With duvet warm
Sheltered from
A rumbling storm.

*But in a country far away
Though a storm may roar,
Where to sleep today, Mum?
On the floor.*

📖 Marjory Francis

❗ Contrast different cultures and expectations

My picnic

Big cakes and bags of crisps,
Squash and lemonade,
Sandwiches with egg and cress,
Or maybe marmalade.
Sweets and biscuits – chocolate ones!
Lollies I can lick.
These are all the things I like
To take on my picnic.

📖 Rose Williams

📖 Luke 9:10-27

❗ An introduction to favourite foods, special meals or eating out of doors themes.

Index

A
A baby for Elizabeth, p44
A daddy and his son, p52
A man with leprosy, p51
Ahab was a greedy, greedy king, p45
All creatures, p9
All creatures great and small, p12
All I need, p87
All together, p31
Alphabet praise, p17
An angel came, p44
Art, p84
At Mamre, p22
At Pentecost, p75
At Simon's house, p52

B
Bartimaeus, p55
Best friends, p91
Body praise! p15
Bold brave Peter? p68
Bread for life, p92

C
Camel ride, p46
Camping out, p86
Can you breathe? p15
Choose some helpers, p74
Christmas animals, p47
'Come and follow me', p49
Come to the church, p78

D
David and Nathan, p34
David is sad, p33
Day and night, p41
Day by day, p87
Do it yourself, p59
Down in Egypt, p27

E
Early in the morning, p50
Easter, p68
Easter morning, p68
Elisha, p38
Esau and Jacob, p24

F
Faithful God, p22
Far away, p47
Feeding the five thousand, p55
Feeling happy, p86
Follow him, p42
'Follow me!', p49
Four busy fishermen, p49
Friends, p89
Friends together, p89

G
Give thanks, p22
Go, go Jonah! p40
God does! p13
God hears, p21
God is good, p41
God is great, p28
God is there! p81
God is with me, p20
God knows and cares, p19
God loves you! p21
God made, p7
God made the earth, p10
God shows his care, p12
God was pleased, p12
God will protect us, p20
God's Spirit, p80
God's story, p32
God's world, p8
Goliath the giant, p32
Goliath was big, p32
Good neighbours? p65
Good news, p43
Good to see you, p89
Great and wonderful, p7
Great wise men, p47

H
Harvest song, p14
He's alive, p70
Hear what God has done, p31
Hello God. It's me. p88
Hello, hello, p91
Helping, p92
Helping and healing, p54
Helping friends, p91
Here and there, p94
Here is Jacob, p24
Here is the church, p73
How things grow, p14

I
I am growing, p82
I don't know, p83
I know, p42
I like books, p86
I will miss them, p34
I will sing your praise, p16
I'm building a house, p93
If God made you, p11
If you know who David is, p33
If you wanna be wise, p85
In the beginning, p6

J
Jacob's dream, p22
Jairus and Jesus, p52
Jeremiah and the potter, p38
Jeremiah and the scroll, p40
Jeremiah in the well, p39
Jesus heals, p50
Jesus is alive! p71
Jesus is always with me, p42
Jesus is it you? p71
Jesus is light, p41
Jesus is the best friend, p45
Jesus listens, p70
Jesus loves us, p43
Jesus shines! p56
Jesus' journey, p67
Jonah, p39
Jump and sing, p42

L
Leaving Egypt, p28
Let the children come, p93
Let's all clap hands! p13
Let's join in! p78
Lights, p8
Lights for the world, p9
Listen to the news, p43
Little seeds, p62
Look up! p48
Looking for the sheep, p63
Looking forward, p61
Love, p55
Lovely bread, p92

M
Manna and water, p30
Mary's gift, p57
Mary's song, p44
Moses, p26
Moses working, p26
Mountain top, p58
Move it! p88
My family, p83
My picnic, p94

N
Naaman in the river, p36
No food, p82
'No', said Pharaoh, p26

O
Obey God, p32
On Easter Day, p71
On the mountain, p36
On tiptoe, p53
Onesimus and Philemon, p80
Only the best, p29
Our Father, p54
Our special friend, p19
Over the Red Sea, p28

P
Paul and Silas, p78
Paul's new friends, p79
Paul's story, p79
Paul's travels, p79
Peter said, p74
Playing, p87
Praise for everything! p16

R
Read the Bible! p78
Receiving, p73
Red ribbons, p66
Rest and rap, p18
Row your boat, p50

S
Sail little boat, p7
Seeds, p63
Seeds and soil, p14
Sharing friends, p90
Shepherds on the hill, p46
Shh! p78
Shine Jesus, p57
Sing a new song, p19
Sing a song of Jacob, p25
So remember, p29
Solomon says, p35
Solomon's wish, p35
Sow the seeds, p14
Star so bright, p48
Stephen, p75
Sunday comes, p61
Superstar! p83

T
Talk to God, p21
Talking to God, p17
Telling the good news, p74
Ten sick men, p56
The angels' song, p46
The donkey's first journey, p66
The farmer and his field, p60
The God of surprises! p19
The greatest treasure, p64
The Holy Spirit, p73
The library, p84
The lost son, p60
The man who was deaf, p54
The potter's house, p38
The promise, p72
The sower, p59
These are the seeds, p62
This and that, p82
This is Good News, p75
This poor man, p51
This way, that way, p76
Three times, p71
Through the desert, p30
Timothy, p80
Trusting God, p20
Two brothers, p23
Two busy fathers, p82
Two friends, p70
Two of us, p83

U
Up popped the seeds, p12

W
Wake up! p56
Watching the wind, p84
We hope you'll stay, p91
We thank you for them all, p9
Weary fishermen, p72
Welcome everybody! p92
What are friends like? p90
What can friends do together? p90
When I'm sad, p87
When we love you, p90
Wherever you are, p13
Who cares? p83
Who listens? p18
Who was there? p25
Who will be a friend? p91
Why, oh why? p81
Will you come? p51
Wise and careless builders, p64
Wise men worship, p48

Y
Yes, yes, yes! p76
You are wonderful! p16
You made the light, p6
You're there! p43